ISBN: 146999254X
ISBN-13: 978-1469992549

CLOUD
SECURITY
AND CONTROL

To my children — Willow, Branson, Avery, and Molly.

TABLE OF CONTENTS

ACKNOWLEDGMENTS

Thank you to Tom Jones, Lee Walker, and Jennifer Allen for their contributions.

1 INTRODUCTION: WHAT IS THE CLOUD?

Cloud computing is a model for enabling convenient, on-demand network access to a shared pool of configurable computing resources ...that can be rapidly provisioned and released with minimal management effort or service provider interaction.

—National Institute of Standards and Technology

The **cloud** is IT infrastructure. Typically, cloud computing refers to a set of services that offer some combination of storage, computation, and applications with efficient scale-up and scale-down capabilities. Cloud computing can refer to public infrastructure, private servers, semi-private resources shared among a limited group, and any hybrid combination thereof.

Because of the buzz surrounding cloud computing, it has come to refer to a broad set of not only services and software but also of concepts and methodologies. For example, to many people, cloud computing represents outsourcing and cost cutting, or at least a shift from capital to operational expenditure. From that perspective, it's easy to see how some people would view cloud computing mostly as a threat while others would see it mostly as an opportunity. Cloud computing has strong detractors, including those who see it as over-hyped and consisting of concepts that aren't new. And cloud computing has strong proponents, including those who see it as an opportunity to accelerate innovation in a bad economy.

Cloud computing is all of those things. But the best way to view the cloud is as one of many tools in your proverbial IT toolbox. For better or worse, the cloud has become a risky tool to ignore. For one thing, misuse of the cloud can lead to expensive mistakes. By the same token, organizations that avoid cloud computing entirely are not only deluding themselves, but they are also very likely missing an opportunity to incorporate capabilities that can give them a competitive advantage.

Security is one of many considerations that organizations encounter early in their exploration of cloud computing. Ironically, when it comes to adoption of cloud computing, many organizations cite perceived security risk as the primary barrier to adoption, when, in fact, return on investment (RoI) is more likely to be the challenge. However, security is also frequently cited as an adoption barrier in a way that is interchangeable with perceived loss of control. Second only to RoI, control should be foremost on the mind of the IT decision maker when planning cloud adoption: who has access to cloud data, resources, and applications, who determines access control, and what tools are in place for managing and auditing access? Notice that those some questions apply regardless of whether the cloud resources are outsourced or on-premises, shared or private. After all, control can be a complex and politically charged issue regardless of the toolset and hosting environment.

Control is an important issue to confront; as with many new and rapidly-changing technology trends, cloud infrastructure is evolving so quickly that the management tools are struggling to keep up.

None of this is intended to diminish the importance of considering the security ramifications of cloud computing. Particularly in regulated industries, missing security requirements can lead to costly fines and lost jobs. The good news is that, when it comes both to control and security, many of the same tools that have served security-conscious organizations successfully for years are just as applicable in this new domain: namely, planning and understanding authentication, authorization, access control, and auditing.

In any technology domain, security has overhead and costs associated with it, and cloud computing is no different. But cloud computing offers some unique opportunities for organizations to use security as a business enabler. For example, many cloud technologies offer ready support for collaboration with partners and customers. Likewise, cloud services are being used by IT organizations to support mobile computing, the "bring your own device" trend, and the consumerization of IT. In all of those contexts, security technologies are an enabler.

2 THE PROS AND CONS OF CLOUD COMPUTING

2.1 Why Should Businesses Invest in the Cloud?

High-growth businesses have advanced IT needs that can only be met by a combination of services and resources that are internal and external, off-premise and on-premises. The most successful businesses are those that can combine those options in innovative ways in order to bring new capabilities to market more quickly and efficiently than their competitors. Compliance requirements and data security sensitivity have so far prevented these businesses from benefitting from public cloud and datacenter colocation.

The ideal solution is one that offers the interoperability of a technology like SQL, the rapid provisioning benefits of the cloud, and the security benefits of on-premises storage. One way to experience these benefits is to turn the typical cloud computing model on its head.

The usual approach to cloud computing is to seek scalability by transitioning front-end compute resources, such as web servers and business logic. However, when it comes to optimizing the competitive benefit gained from line of business application development, front-end scalability is rarely the determining factor. Instead, the most important issue is often the speed at which the new capability (i.e. the app itself) can be deployed, followed by the speed (and associated cost) at which the app can be modified and redeployed as business needs evolve.

In our experience, provisioning new structured storage capacity in the cloud is much quicker than provisioning new structured storage capacity on-premises. This is not to fault on-premises IT personnel. Again, SQL Server is a useful example: it is a complex and full-featured application, and it is time-consuming to support, configure, and maintain. In addition, many IT organizations require that SQL is run on dedicated hardware, rather than on virtual machines. As a result, requests for additional capacity must also provide budget for both equipment and personnel. However, by taking advantage of specialized cloud-based services like SQL Azure or the SQL support in Amazon Web Services, some of that overhead is avoided and, most importantly, deployment can be considerably quicker.

A similar argument can be made about provisioning front-end servers in the cloud versus on-premises. However, in terms of both overhead and deployment speed, the difference isn't nearly as notable as it is for SQL. Therefore, if you have a three tier line of business (LOB) app, and you can only put one tier in the cloud, we recommend that you choose the backend. (We'll come back to that in a second.)

So, cloud-based services such as SQL can be useful for speedy line of business deployment, but how should you secure the data? To ensure data security, one option is to keep front-end app servers on-premises. By performing encryption and decryption within the on-premises application server, you only store encrypted data in SQL, and plaintext data never reaches the cloud. With this "secured cloud and on-premises" mixed solution, you still get all of the benefits of SQL with the flexibility of cloud storage.

2.2 Benefits and Risks

By now everyone has heard about the incredible benefits of cloud computing: the ability to scale up or scale down capacity as needs demand, the replacement of capital expenditures with operational expenditures, and the broad reach across oceans and continents.

With any new technology, however, it's natural for organizations to be concerned about new problems that they might encounter by adopting it. The industry has been mostly focused so far on manageability and reliability, with security concerns mostly targeted to authentication of the user to the cloud ecosystem. However, whenever any function is moved to a remote server, criminals will try to subvert either the remote server or the client's connection to it.

Putting any enterprise assets into the cloud exposes them to new attacks from the Internet. Fortunately, the attacks against cloud resources have been addressed by cloud providers. For example, an October 2011 *Technology Review* article (see the resources at the end of this chapter) detailed an attack that was made possible by the co-location of virtual machines (VMs) in a cloud environment. This vulnerability was discovered and fixed before it was exploited, but still highlights a potential real-world threat. Security researchers and attackers will find similar vulnerabilities over the coming years, and these vulnerabilities will be fixed. There have already been threat analyses of virtualization schemes that are used by most cloud providers, including private clouds; however, the particular problems of moving services from an internal network to the Internet have yet to be adequately examined.

IT organizations are gearing up for security that is not dependent on an impregnable boundary perimeter between the Internet and the enterprise network, (also known as **de-perimeterization**). The public cloud is the ultimate realization of de-perimeterization. Criminals have yet to perfect their techniques for exploiting enterprise data in the public cloud; however, that will soon change. Attackers have already completed simple attacks, such as using fraudulent websites to exploit simple problems, such as customers accidentally typing the wrong URL for a company or an attacker confusing customers with a legitimate-appearing phishing email with non-Latin characters in the company's URL. Unfortunately, the ecosystem's current attempts to fix these attacks with Extended Validation SSL certificates and DNS-SEC have had little impact. While those approaches give consumers the information needed to make correct decisions, only a fraction of users will understand and use them, in part, because so few sites today are using techniques to provide this verification to the user.

Attacks against servers are not new. For example, the original release of Microsoft Terminal Services did not require TLS authentication or encryption of the client's link to the server. This lack of encryption allowed attackers to take advantage of a man-in-the-middle attack to intercept and read RDP traffic between the client and the server. Once the vulnerability was discovered, Microsoft quickly added TLS support. We are now in a similar situation with the cloud—if enterprise resources are in the cloud, attackers can use various social engineering tactics to lure enterprise users to bogus sites that appear to be legitimate. Because detailed threat analyses have not been created for the entire cloud infrastructure, these vulnerabilities are not being mitigated in most deployments. To be fully secure, each new cloud infrastructure should be methodically analyzed for potential vulnerabilities. At JW Secure, we have found threat modeling to be an easy win for gaining customer confidence and helping to restore a sense of control because of the visibility that the analysis yields.

> ### IS VIRTUALIZATION A SECURITY BOUNDARY?
>
> NetworkWorld recently ran an article noting how VMWare has begun to virtualize Android smartphones for business users. This might lead the casual reader to conclude that VMware believes that virtualization is indeed a security boundary.
>
> Admittedly, there's a semantic debate here. However, there is credible research indicating that, if virtualization is a security boundary, it's not a very good one.

To learn more about the concepts discussed in this article, see the following pages. These pages are also posted on the resources page for this book at JWSecure.com/CloudSecurityBook.

- **Security Researchers Rain on Amazon's Cloud**
  tinyurl.com/6p3bjh5
  Technology Review | MIT's Technology Review on the threats of co-location.

- **Extended Validation SSL**
  tinyurl.com/7s583t6
  VeriSign | VeriSign provides details about a new certificate that can give consumers more confidence.

- **Configure authentication and encryption on terminal server**
  tinyurl.com/885dfkh
  Microsoft | Details how to enable encryption (this is not the default setting for Windows Terminal Services).

- **Microsoft RDP Server Private Key Disclosure**
  tinyurl.com/6qs46mq
  Microsoft | Details the terminal server vulnerability are discussed in this article (this issue was patched soon after it was disclosed).

3 CLOUD APPLICATION DESIGN

3.1 Application Design

The financial model for cloud computing seems like an irresistible option for meeting budget pressures. After consuming services, you're billed on a monthly basis, which means that the cloud computing services are considered an operational expense, not a capital expense.

You can reduce overhead by consolidating resources into large shared datacenters. This creates efficiencies in staffing and power consumption. You can scale your service usage up or down as you need—no overcapacity and no lost opportunity.

Finally, there are multiple ways that broadly deployed cloud-based applications can support your business needs. You can prepare for and account for an increasingly mobile workforce, a diverse collection of business partners, and a worldwide supply chain.

While the cost and collaboration benefits might be obvious, the road to the cloud is not without its potholes, many of which are hidden. You'll have to retrain your IT staff, create new requisition and operations processes, and update data security and compliance policies. Fortunately, you can address these challenges in a systematic way. This chapter provides a look at the major decision points that a typical organization will face when taking its first line of business project to an Internet-based cloud provider.

3.1.1   Get Started

Business managers are always looking for applications to help them run their businesses more efficiently—whether it's for analyzing data for faster decision making or for getting greater visibility into business operations. And whether those capabilities come from commercial or customized apps, the burden is on IT to deliver and operate an ever-expanding set of services under continuous budget pressure.

When a business application is completely stand-alone with no compliance or security constraints, the consideration for cloud hosting is greatly simplified to the cost of deployment and operation. Most business applications will require a more careful risk-and-benefit analysis before deciding how to manage cloud hosting:

1. Authentication methods for both public and private (enterprise) users.

2. Security threats and mitigations when using the public cloud.

3. Compliance regulations, and how to simplify adherence to the policies them by using the right architecture.

The first two considerations have common solutions for most deployments, and compliance regulations depend on the location and type of data to be handled by the app. The major compliance issues, roughly in order of decreasing complexity, are:

1. Government regulations prohibiting personal or national secrets from crossing international boundaries.

2. Health information protected by HIPAA or similar regulations.

3. Identity theft. In particular, release of access to financial accounts.

4. Public disclosure of a user's Personally Identifiable Information (PII).

5. Internal requirements for handling of business-sensitive data.

3.1.2 Authentication Issues

Some cloud service users won't be part of a corporate directory like Microsoft's Active Directory. In that case, the cloud service needs to aggregate users from different **identity providers (IdPs)**. These will have potentially different access rules to the cloud resources.

When there are both public and private (within the enterprise) users, cloud apps will require access to access and policy data. Therefore, you could conveniently deploy that data to the cloud. This type of deployment will permit access from any type of device, even if that device isn't part of the enterprise directory.

You'll probably end up moving old data into the new database for cloud hosting, but handling the schema mapping and data migration should be no different than any other migration. There are tools that make the identity federation process easier. However, there could also be compliance issues associated with the data in either the database or the cloud resources.

Claims mapping is a useful approach for onboarding different applications consuming federated identities. For example, the Windows Azure Access Control Service (http://tinyurl.com/75wywna) is a cloud service that can aggregate claims from an on-premises Active Directory Federation Services (ADFS) server and external IdPs (Windows Live, Facebook, Google, etc.). Using cloud services for identity aggregation gives you support for many programming languages and many existing IdPs.

By mapping, or translating, claims generated by ADFS, for example, to claims customized for a given on-or-off-premises application, you reduce application complexity and maintenance costs. This approach mediates the relationship between on-premises users, cloud resources, and users accessing the data from the Internet (see **Figure 1**).

Figure 1 - Claims mapping - Mediating between on-premises and cloud resources

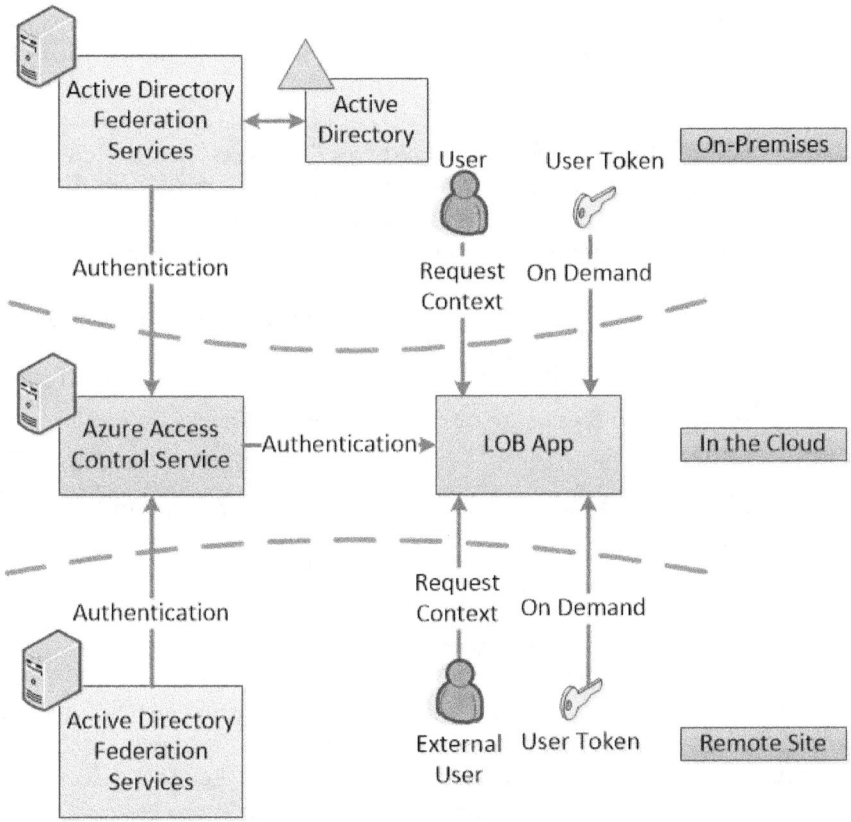

3.1.3   Public Cloud Security Threats

Few organizations can afford the same critical mass of IT personnel, expertise, and processes as the major cloud infrastructure providers. And experience has demonstrated that you can run some apps more securely in the cloud than on-premises.

However, there will be new threats introduced as a result of public Internet connections. These types of threats are introduced by network de-perimeterization, and you'll need to address them eventually anyway. Still, new public cloud deployments should be subject to security review. You should take the following considerations into account.

- **Domain Restrictions.** Within the enterprise domain, specify that only domain-joined computers are permitted. You can use mechanisms like Network Access Protection (NAP) and IPsec to ensure that all machines are well-known and managed against security threats. You can also extend these mechanisms into the cloud.

- **Cloud Service SLAs.** Cloud-based servers are covered by service-level agreements (SLAs), which you must include in a security review. You need to ensure that uptime, security, privacy, and compliance certifications are satisfactorily addressed.

You should also consider the following specific attack points when completing your security review:

- Information disclosure or denial-of-service attacks on public traffic.

- Man-in-the-middle spoofing of either cloud or on-premises servers.

- Hijacking existing connections on the public Internet.

- Replay of cloud credentials.

These types of attacks have all been seen in prior generations of enterprise services. You can use the data flow to analyze threats introduced when a public cloud is used with on-premises services (see **Figure 2** below). You should analyze the following three basic types of connections.

1. **Neither end of the connection is at a trusted location**. There's no way to evaluate the connection, so any claim from the IdP in this example must be digitally signed by the service to ensure integrity of the message.

2. **One end of the connection is in the cloud**. The other is at a user site that is not managed by the enterprise. In this case, you can protect the connection with an SSL (TLS or HTTPS) link where credentials can be provided to either (or both) ends of the link to ensure some level of authentication, as well as data protection while transiting the cloud. Without a verifiable identity at each end, man-in-the-middle attacks are possible.

3. **Both ends of the connection are in a trusted location.**
Because the cloud might not be under control of the enterprise, strong identity at both ends is also required. In this example either SSL or IPsec (VPN) connections will provide the protections needed.

Figure 2 - Analyze the threats to your data before taking action

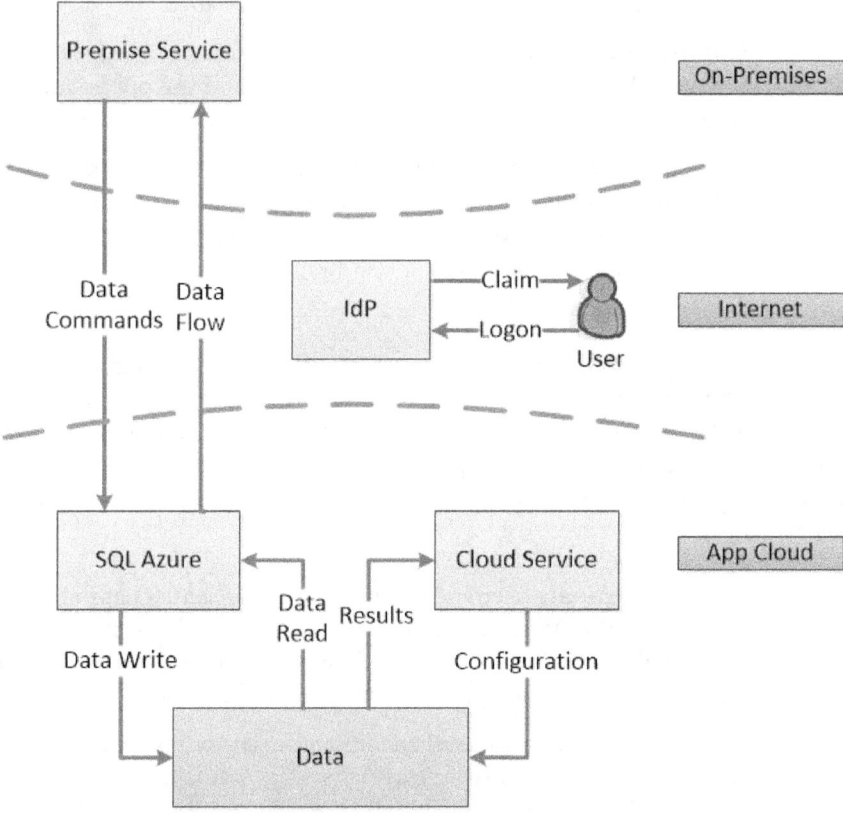

3.1.4   Architect for Compliance

You might not be able to determine how auditors will classify data before an application is ready for deployment. Even worse, data classification could change, even after the app is deployed. Compliance auditors prefer to conduct a finished app audit before the app is deployed, but that can be expensive. Instead of holding up a deployment while waiting for clarity on the requirements, it's easier to institute compensating controls to avoid compliance problems. These methods can help you avoid compliance issues with cloud deployments:

1. **Ensure a good separation of control.** This suggests that any process that can access sensitive data should not also be accessible to the Internet. If some Internet-facing process needs the data, try to locate the sensitive data separately from the non-sensitive data, even if they're accessed by the same key.

2. **Control data protocol design.** Make sure data protocols between the apps that handle sensitive data and the public-facing apps are designed so they can't accommodate sensitive data.

3. **Use encryption to protect sensitive data.** Decryption keys shouldn't be accessible to public-facing apps. You can deploy sensitive keys and apps in the cloud or on-premises, but they should never have the same access permissions as publically accessible apps.

When you have to release data to users on the public Internet, separate the line of business app from the compliance engine that will handle all the access and audit checks for sensitive data. These data flows illustrate that architecture (see **Figure 3**). This might appear complex, but there are only two major concepts you need to understand regarding separation of control:

1. You can aggregate user authentication with a claims mapping service like the Windows Azure AC Service. This collects user credentials from an on-premises federated Active Directory and a cloud-based IdP, such as Windows Live or Facebook.

2. Separate the components of the line of business application that handle protected data from those that don't, enabling compliance auditing efforts to focus on the former.

Figure 3 - Any compliance checks should be handled independent of the line-of-business apps

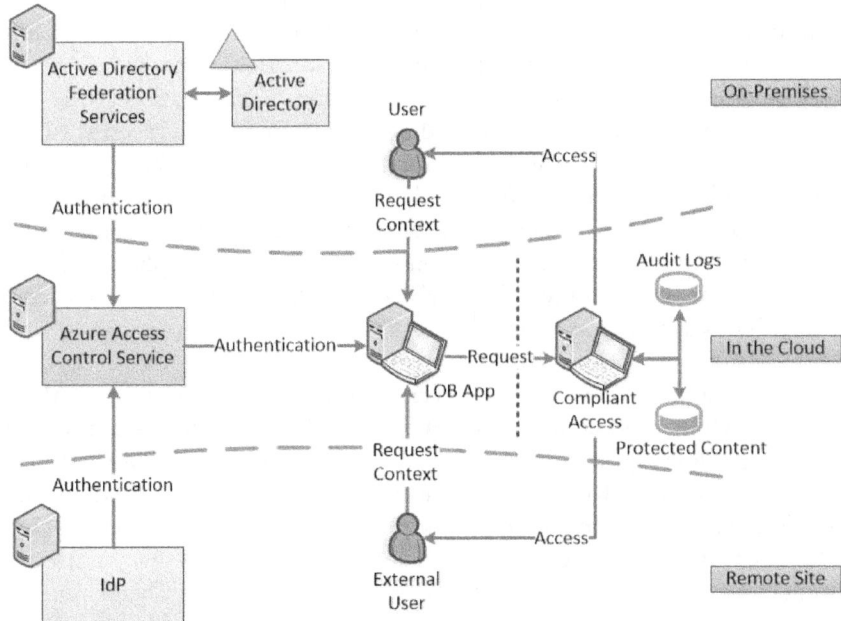

Now, you'll need to determine where you'll locate the compliance access engine. You could have the compliance engine hosted in the cloud for operational efficiency, or on-premises for enhanced security. You have to protect all connections that carry sensitive data.

We've explored four solutions here for moving into the cloud. Each solution addresses specific application needs or vulnerabilities. Your first step is to understand what data you'll have to expose on the public Internet. If that's sensitive data, user authentication is critical. If it isn't, then separating data and control might avoid any compliance issues.

Once you make these choices, draw out a preliminary data flow diagram and look at the attack points. Taken together, this preparation should give you the confidence you need to tackle a line of business cloud deployment.

3.2 Claims Mapping

Claims mapping is an important technique for improving the maintainability of applications offering federated authentication. Claims mapping does this by abstracting the details of identity provider-specific semantics. Suppose that you are federating authorization with two separate organizations, each exposed by their own ADFS server. It's likely that the ADFS servers, and the claims issued by each, are configured slightly differently. Suppose further that you have two separate but related applications, both of which must be accessible to both organizations. Claims mapping allows you to not only isolate that two applications from the variations between the two ADFS servers, but to also output claims in a way that is application-specific.

For example, one ADFS server might issue a claim of **Title = Doctor**, while another server might issue a claim of **Title = Dr**. Claims mapping allows canonicalization of those titles. Further, if one application is used to track drug dispensation and one is used to view medical records, the former could implemented to expect a claim such as **MayPrescribe** and the other a claim such as **MayView**. With this implementation, the logic of interpreting titles has been entirely abstracted from the application, resulting in less duplication of logic and in code that is easier to understand and maintain.

The Windows Azure Access Control Service is one of the most notable solutions today offering claims mapping.

3.3 Data Security

Cloud security faces two challenges. The first is data sovereignty. For example, an American company must conform to American data sovereignty laws. This general concept applies worldwide, of course. Those laws determine, for example, who is able to demand access to that data, and when and why they're permitted to access it. A particular government, and the private sector entities that support it, are unlikely to want to store data on a foreign cloud service since the foreign government could seize it whenever it wants. Cloud infrastructure providers have responded to this concern by providing software and services for creating and managing private clouds.

The second security challenge is data encryption. In the <u>Crypto Services and Data Security in Windows Azure</u> article on MSDN (tinyurl.com/7d4s4eg), Jonathan Wiggins mentions that the threat of data compromise from within the cloud. To mitigate that threat, the article suggests creating and storing keys in the cloud. However, that's not going to work if someone from within the cloud compromises your keys, or compromises whatever secret protects those keys. The only solution is to store the secret outside of the cloud and never transmit it to the cloud. That greatly limits the scalability benefit of the cloud – which is supposed to be one of its main selling points – unless all you're looking for is pure storage space.

Let's be realistic, though – applications are being migrated to the cloud. To that end, we recommend that you review JD Meier's blog post about Azure Security (tinyurl.com/6rhptfv) which links to a detailed paper. The paper offers some useful threat modeling checklists in the References section at the end. For example, see the section entitled "Cheat Sheet - Web Application Security Threats and Countermeasures at a Glance", starting on page 86. Although these points are directed at Microsoft's cloud platform, they are generally applicable to other public cloud offerings.

3.4 Security Must-Haves

According to Gartner, cloud computing providers need to build security features into their offerings from the ground up, but allow them to be controlled and dialed-in separately from other infrastructure features. This is an easy concept that is hard to execute.

Interestingly, on one hand, there is a correlation between those features. For example, if my cloud hosted application is accessible to the Internet, I'll want a certain type of security configuration. But if the app is intended to be accessible only to a certain on-premises server, I'll want a different security configuration.

In the general case, it would be convenient for the provider to offer sensible defaults to use for common scenarios. But that brings us to the other hand: there are indeed common scenarios (hosted SharePoint with single sign-on for employee access), but there is rarely a one-size-fits-all option (oh, I need to federate, and did I mention that some of the data is public and some is export-controlled?).

Rich application programming interfaces (.NET, Java) have offered that kind of flexibility for years, but there's an interesting difference now.

For example, with a web app running on-premises, the line of business development team writes it and the IT group configures the server. But with that same web app running in a hosted cloud fabric, the line of business dev team writes it and the line of business team uses the fabric's web service API to configure it. Or the IT team does that.

In other words, you've got application developers and configuration developers, but no IT operations people. Or are they now operations developers? Or is it just another name for the same thing?

3.5 Cloud Data Encryption Case Study: SecurEntity

The open-source SecurEntity project (tinyurl.com/88ygtuq) grew out of an ongoing engagement we (JW Secure) have with a Fortune 100 company. We needed to develop a custom line of business application relating to the management of IT security exceptions. From an implementation perspective, a SQL based solution for storing the application data was appropriate, but there's a major bureaucratic hurdle in that approach: SQL requires the provisioning of new onsite physical hardware (not a virtual machine), a place in the datacenter to put it, and a commitment for 24/7 infrastructure support. None of those three things was going to be available in the timeframe requested by the line of business team.

SQL in the cloud was the obvious alternative, but we had to meet the security bar for offsite storage of sensitive data. Thus, this is one half of what SecurEntity does: implement a proxy to handle encryption and decryption between an onsite application server and cloud-based SQL instance in a way that's transparent to the application code.

It's our belief that the encrypting proxy alone would be sufficient to meet the formal security requirement (i.e., data must be encrypted) that most organizations will apply when in a similar situation. However, careful analysis shows that encryption alone isn't enough to ensure that the data can't be maliciously tampered with in subtle ways. For example, by swapping two encrypted rows in the database, could a malicious administrator at the cloud data center affect our IT security line of business application in such a way that an unwanted policy change becomes enacted?

The second half of the SecurEntity solution mitigates that threat by performing a cryptographic integrity check on each object, and the objects they reference, each time they're read from the cloud.

This is an important consideration: encryption alone does not make your data tamper proof. Currently, application-layer solutions such as SecurEntity are the only way to both protect your cloud data from malicious tampering, as well as from unwanted disclosure.

4 THE CLOUD IS ALL ABOUT CONTROL

When our children were young, we kept them safe at home. When they had learned to fend for themselves, we let them venture forth. It's a similar situation with enterprise assets. We've traditionally protected them within the perimeter of the network. We put up firewalls to ensure those assets didn't leave the premises.

When you tell an IT manager he can share his local computing load with on-demand cloud-based resources, the first reaction is excitement at the possible cost savings and user experience improvements. But like an overprotective parent, that excitement often turns to skepticism and anxiety about the new challenges of securing enterprise assets across multiple control points.

Data processing has already moved from the enterprise datacenter to PCs spread across the world. The next logical step is to move the enterprise data and applications from within the enterprise firewall to where they'll be closer to the business users who need them. That means moving to the cloud.

To reap the benefits of cloud computing without the accompanying anxiety, you need to establish distributed access control to match the distributed content and applications. Here, we'll outline the steps you need to take to ensure reliability and control as your data and applications move beyond the enterprise perimeter.

Secure Your Cloud Architecture: Step-by-Step

1. Establish a service-oriented architecture (SOA) to ensure that you can safely relocate each component.

2. Centralize the management of data and application deployment and updates.

3. Use federated identity management processes to ensure every user is known at every point in the cloud.

19

4. Assign roles and other attributes to each user to verify data-access claims.

5. Assign access-control rules to applications and data that can move with them to the cloud.

6. Authorize access to applications and data based on verified user-access claims.

4.1 Service-Oriented Architecture

The first step in establishing an anxiety-free cloud deployment is to create a diagram showing the application and the data flow between the components. For the design to be service-oriented, each application needs to operate as a service that users can access either locally or in the cloud. Similarly for data, the location of the data should not be specified in the application. You need to be able to configure that location when you deploy the application. You can see in the figure below how the components of the IT environment relate with the applications and data sourced on either local or cloud resources.

Figure 4 - Architecture of Application and Data Flows

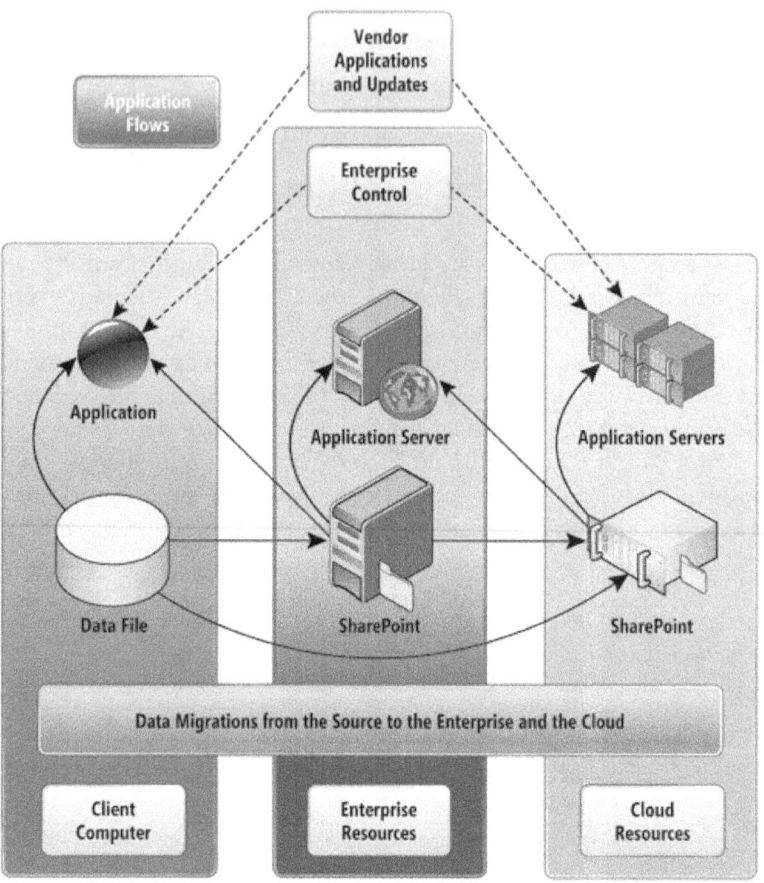

Your development team sources the application executable files. You can have them apply those directly from the vendor, but you can exert more control if you first bring all application code and updates into the enterprise and have it distributed from there. Data migrates from the client machine to either the enterprise or cloud data stores, which are shown as SharePoint servers in **Figure 4**.

When applications access data, that action is authorized by access-control mechanisms local to each data store. The integrity of the application executable files and the enterprise data needs extra consideration as it moves beyond the perimeter and into the cloud. The ideal and most flexible management situation is when you can manage local and cloud resources as a single entity that can dynamically respond to resource requests.

4.2 Accounting for the Cloud

The first step in justifying any cloud deployment is determining the return on investment. You typically classify cost as set-up or conversion that includes commissioning the new services, training, and decommissioning the old services. Return is expressed as reduced cost-per-month and the number of months to recoup the investment. More sophisticated analysis includes discounted cash flow analysis, but if the return is less than two years, that likely adds no real value to the decision process.

The real value of cloud deployments comes from intangible benefits such as improved responsiveness to fluctuations in demand for services and improved cost control. Consider these types of costs from the perspective of the IT department:

1. Fixed costs typically come from investments in capital equipment like servers and machine rooms. The costs are typically depreciated over the lifetime of the asset. That depreciation will be charged to the income statement every month regardless of the equipment use.

2. Variable costs depend on the amount of service provided and will include cost of goods sold and any fee charged based on cloud usage, such as short-term equipment rental based on the current load. This type of cost gives the IT department the best ability to tie costs to service delivery.

3. Semi-variable costs typically come from services provided to full-time employees or other resources that are more difficult to scale up or scale down. Software rental or provisioning e-mail services will be in this category. The inertia behind provisioning and de-provisioning employees causes this cost to significantly lag behind changes in demand for services.

You can justify using cloud services for semi-variable costs for reasons such as off-loading payroll services to a dedicated provider. In payroll, as in e-mail, the rules change rapidly—the software needs constant updates and the expertise to perform these functions is expensive. While it's more difficult to justify cloud provisioning based on semi-variable costs, the results can still be positive and can help IT focus on the real mission of delivering value to the enterprise products.

4.3 Four Steps to a Secure Cloud Deployment

Most IT executives think cloud computing is a way to reduce capital expenditures by using virtualization technology (tinyurl.com/82hqq52). Many vendors tack the word "cloud" onto any Internet service. For our purposes here, we're using the Gartner, Inc. description (http://tinyurl.com/5zmwd2) of how the cloud came to be so important to business: "the commoditization and standardization of technologies, in part to virtualization and the rise of service-oriented software architectures, and most importantly, to the dramatic growth in popularity of the Internet."

This is important in four specific areas:

1. Centralized data management, using SharePoint as an example.

2. Centralized application management, using Exchange as an example.

3. Federated identity management, using Active Directory Federation Services (ADFS) as an example.

4. Additional assistance for migrating to the cloud.

4.3.1 Centralized Data Management

In 2007, Gartner began telling security conferences that it was time to abandon the hardened perimeter boundary between the enterprise and the Internet. Even at that time, experts were arguing that enterprise boundaries were already porous. Perimeters had become irrelevant to the task of keeping out intruders, so access control was required with every IT service. Security de-perimeterization is the current reality. To be truly secure, only the server that contains data can ultimately control access.

Still, it isn't rational to manage access at every server, because many deployments contain hundreds or even thousands of servers. IT can't really determine data rights and access rules. IT can, however, establish a role-management system with which business owners can permit or deny access relevant to business objectives.

The regulatory environment has become increasingly stringent both for data modification and data access. This requires a new paradigm: one that will allow data to migrate to whichever server is best able to service access requests, while ensuring compliance at reasonable cost. Here are some requirements to consider for data management in a cloud environment:

- Fast access to data for which the user is authorized, and when and where it is required.

- Access not compromised by a natural or business catastrophe.

- Data discovery by legal governmental requests, assuming the enterprise can provide the data needed.

- Data Loss Prevention (DLP) is an integral part of the service offering.

- A service-oriented architecture (SOA) should enable easy data migration back and forth to the cloud.

- Identity of data must not include its physical location, so that the data can easily be moved.

- Location tags for data should be the logical country of origin, not the data's physical location.

- Data backup and recovery operations need to be based on the data identity, not its location.

- Data-access rules can be created and maintained by the business owner of the data.

- Access permissions can be viewed by compliance auditors.

- Sensitive data can have audit controls for both modification and access.

- Separation of duties prevents the same administrator from modifying data and audit logs.

- SLAs need to spell out everyone's expectations and responsibilities.

4.3.1.1 Data Management Case Study: Starbucks

Starbucks Corp. found that the cost and delay of physical (paper-based) distribution of current pricing, business analysis and news was not cost-effective. As a result, it now supports SharePoint for its network of 16,000 locations. That SharePoint site has become a business-critical communications channel through which employees can get current information, with the ability to search quickly for the information that they need, when they need it.

Starbucks tracks availability and reliability is with Microsoft System Center Operations Manager (SCOM) (tinyurl.com/6rqf3qv) and other analytic tools. Because SharePoint supports both internal and external network connections, the server locations can adapt to suit the current network topology without concern for local, cloud or mixed environments. This deployment has enabled Starbucks to realize the following benefits:

- Supporting store growth and capacity needs by improving system stability with effective monitoring and reporting tools.

- Allowing store partners to work more efficiently and effectively with an intuitive portal interface and easy access to information across the enterprise.

- Maintaining data security with enhanced document management and privacy functionality.

- Aligning store priorities with company objectives by integrating trends and growth reports with partner communications.

4.3.1.2 Integrity Protection

Any data store must be prevented from becoming an infection vector for viruses or spyware. Data types, like executables and compressed or encrypted files, can be blocked for a variety of integrity and compliance concerns. Microsoft employee David Tesar blogged about some of the business reasons (http://tinyurl.com/7v2nsjx) to protect SharePoint using Forefront Protection 2010 for SharePoint.

4.3.1.3 Data Loss Protection and Detection

To ensure full protection, data from one customer must be properly segregated from that of another. It must be stored securely when "at rest" and able to move securely from one location to another (security "in motion"). IT managers must ensure that cloud providers have systems in place to prevent data leaks or access by third parties. This should be part of an SLA. Proper separation of duties should ensure that unauthorized users can't defeat auditing and/or monitoring—even "privileged" users at the cloud provider. The following figure shows the various data transitions susceptible to outside attack.

Figure 5 – The relationship of data and trust transitions

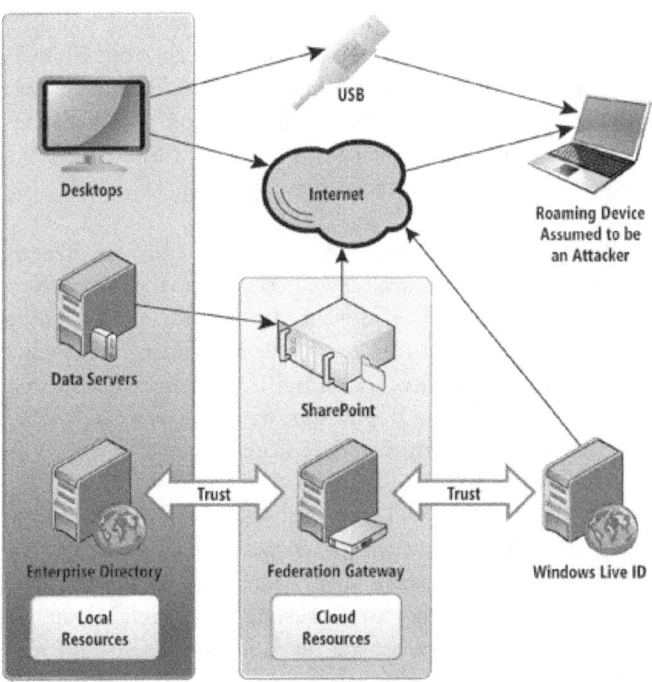

The new attack points against enterprise desktops and servers using the Internet or physical media include:

1. Data transfers from the enterprise to the cloud, losing authorization information in transit.

2. Cloud accesses to cloud SharePoint services that don't have enterprise protection.

3. Private data leakage or data leakage of authorization information from external ID providers.

As the amount of data increases, the time to filter this data or the cost to increase storage capacity can be significant. The data keyword and file-filtering available with Forefront Protection 2010 for SharePoint lets you control the type of data you allow on the SharePoint server and provide reporting on what types of files are present. This functionality can reduce costs by not requiring additional storage capacity and by helping to prevent data leaks.

For instance, if you have a publicly accessible SharePoint server in your company, you can enable keyword file-filtering to prevent anything with the words "confidential" or "internal only" inside the files. You can even specify the threshold of how many times these words show up before you disallow them from being posted.

Rights Management Services (RMS) is also an effective addition to your defense-in-depth strategy, protecting the documents themselves regardless of where they're stored or downloaded. Most commercial applications don't need this level of protection, but it can be helpful for some particularly sensitive documents, like financial or acquisition plans prior to public release. Beginning with the release of Windows Server 2008, RMS is a role in Active Directory.

A full audit trail will be required for any forensic investigation, resulting in a huge amount of data. You can enable Audit Collection Services (ACS), an add-in for Microsoft System Center Operations Manager (SCOM), on high-risk resources to pull all of the audit records as they're generated to a central place for secure storage and analysis. This configuration will prevent attackers from tampering with the forensic data, even if the attackers have high privilege.

The "Trust" arrow in **Figure 5** above indicates this important flow of authentication and authorization information, explored later in this article in the section Federated Identity Management.

4.3.1.4 Centralized Health-Care Data Management

Major players vying for a slice of the medical information market include Microsoft Health Vault (tinyurl.com/3zfrltw) and Dossia (tinyurl.com/avke54). Dossia, an independent nonprofit infrastructure created by some of the largest employers in the United States, gathers and stores information for lifelong health records.

President Obama raised the expectation of benefits from centralized health-care data in the United States in terms of reduced costs and improvements in research. With the Health Insurance Portability and Accountability Act legislation, there's also enormous pressure to protect patient privacy. Medical information is sensitive and has enormous impact that can change people's lives if, for example, it's used in employment decisions.

Questions have already been raised on the use of genetic markers in employment decisions. Congress addressed those questions in the Genetic Information Non-Discrimination Act (tinyurl.com/5sr4gw). The next several years will see the tension escalate between cost containment and privacy as cloud service providers try to navigate this minefield.

While employers have an incentive to reduce health-care costs, it's important to understand the security model: who collects the data, how is the data used, who has access to the data, and what are the risks of collecting and sharing the data? One interesting question in the context of cloud computing is, who's responsible when there's a problem? Who's the custodian of the record and what happens if there's a significant data breach or misuse? As sensitive information such as medical records move into the cloud, security concerns will certainly escalate.

4.3.2   Centralized Application Management

Web-hosting applications have been outsourced for at least a decade. During that time, Akamai has hosted an increasingly large percentage of time-critical files for website owners worldwide. Also, programmer Dave Winer worked with Microsoft to create the precursor (tinyurl.com/6sb7vle) to the Web services that have proliferated to the wide range of WS-* standards that are available today (tinyurl.com/7dkfpas).

Web-based applications have steadily grown in importance, to the point where a new name seemed necessary for the combination of service-orientation and standardized Internet service interfaces—hence the term "cloud computing." What's new and different today from 10 years ago is the attention given to the value that's available at a reasonable marginal cost. A company no longer needs to develop Exchange expertise to have the benefit of Exchange services, as there are a number of vendors competing to provide that service.

For a service to migrate easily from a local location to the cloud and back again, the application needs to provide a standard service-oriented set of interfaces for use both locally and in the cloud. This is why a cloud application was initially called software as a service. The most widely adopted application-service interface standards are the WS-* protocols mentioned earlier. When a business application is undergoing a revision, it's a good time to include time to review the application-interface specifications to see if they can fit one of the existing Web services standards.

All authorization claims and authentication identity need to be shared by all resources, whether local or cloud-based (tinyurl.com/7m2arhy). Over time, all applications will become able to migrate to the most efficient locale to meet their customers' expectations. At that point, moving an application is a simple matter of changing a directory entry for the application. Provisioning resources is just a base functionality of the services provider selected. The cloud provides a virtualized view of the resources that looks like a single computer, one that's never down for services, but could in reality be hosted on many machines or shared on a single machine, as demand requires.

Any application provider needs to ensure that it doesn't become an infection vector for malware. E-mail providers are especially attractive vectors for malware distribution, but attacks can almost be guaranteed through any channel with a public component. Forefront Protection 2010 for Exchange Server gives users of cloud-hosted applications the confidence that no other customer will compromise services that that they depend upon. All executables are checked before they can be loaded onto the servers and into client computers.

4.3.3 Federated Identity Management

Online identity has two primary manifestations these days:

1. **Government or corporations insist on a tight binding between human identity and online identity**. The rise of machine-readable passports and government-issued smart cards is proof of that assertion. Active Directory is one example of this type of support.

2. **Online ID providers supply a consistent identity used to build a profile for predicting future behavior.** Windows Live ID operating on the Internet with simple Turing tests (such as CAPTCHA) proves that a human being is requesting the account. A simpler example is a verification code sent to an Internet e-mail account.

Depending on the application, either one or both types of identity might be provided to the cloud service to obtain authorization to access data. Every enterprise will have its own identity-management system to control access to information and computing resources (tinyurl.com/85mvtcb). That identity should have the same weight for getting authorization to run applications in the cloud.

External identity providers will typically only verify customers or other casual users. Therefore, the cloud identity system needs to track the owner of each identity and the level of assurance that's given to that identity. Coexistence of services in local and cloud environments is only possible when the same standard service identity interface is used for authorization in both environments.

Only a few enterprises will be interested in creating their own private cloud service. For those doing so, the cloud identity solution will need to work across all divisions and acquisitions. While it's possible for a cloud service to create its own identity provider, such a proprietary solution would take it outside of our definition of a true cloud service.

These cases would need a federation gateway from each cloud service to link the external identity to an internal identity manager, such as Forefront Identity Manager, to provide a clean and quick authorization provider for each cloud resource completely independent of the original identity provider. Identity providers must create a list of all known sources of identity used to authorize access to resources to be sure that any cloud services provider can accommodate all of them.

4.3.3.1 Using Federated Identity

As reported in the Forefront team blog, Thomson Reuters was able to provide single sign-on (SSO) access to its Treasura treasury management and related cloud services (http://tinyurl.com/7exra9b). The firm used federated identity management based on ADFS 2.0 from its customers' corporate logon identity without having to sign in again to access the Thomson Reuters products.

Among the many identity providers supported by Treasura are Sun OpenSSO and Microsoft Active Directory. Because Windows Identity Foundation provides its application developers with the same familiar Windows development tools to provide SSO without having to write custom authentication code, Thomson Reuters expects to save an average of three months of development time.

The easiest approach to cloud authentication is exposing access only through the company's own identity provider. That approach works as long as any user tracking is limited to the use of the company's identity provider. As soon as customers or other partners need to have controlled access to the cloud applications or data, the enterprise is going to need a heterogeneous source of user identity. Sometimes the identity will be strong—such as national identity smart cards—but in other cases it will just provide continuity like Windows Live ID.

The end-point application and data servers will need to be aware of the origin and reliability of the identity presented in such heterogeneous environments before authorizing access. Thus, for example, business-critical information can be protected with the enterprise's own Active Directory while the external identity provider can be used for tracking customer behavior over an extended period.

ADFS is part of the Microsoft identity and security platform, as well as part of its Windows Azure cloud operating environment. ADFS, a Windows Server component, provides Web SSO technologies to authenticate a user to multiple Web applications.

ADFS 2.0 is designed to allow users to employ SSO across both cloud-hosted and on-premises applications. This gives Microsoft Online Services the ability to authenticate with corporate ID from Active Directory or Windows Live IDs. Cloud administrators will still need to have a separate ID for that functionality. ADFS 2.0, together with Windows Identity Foundation, was been known in the past by its code name "Geneva."

4.3.4   Cloud Migration Assistance

There are several ways you can get help as your organization prepares to migrate to the cloud, including vendor support, security services, availability, application security, elasticity, management, privacy, and private cloud services:

- **Vendor Support.** Companies specializing in enterprise security have the expertise to evaluate the many new concerns as companies migrate to cloud-computing services. Any qualified cloud-security expert will be able to create checklists and templates that enterprises can then use as they roll out new services. Be sure to create a list of requirements for any vendor that includes developing SOA to address specific security needs for the enterprise. It's important that vendors have security expertise, as well as experience deploying secure solutions in real-world environments. Specific experience with major cloud providers like Microsoft, Google, and Amazon will translate into a plan that can help ensure success.

- **Physical and Personnel Security.** Providers need to ensure that physical machines are adequately secure. They must also ensure that access to these machines, as well as all customer data, is not only restricted but documented. The U.S. Government Accountability Office (GAO) has published a document on the *Knowledge of Software Suppliers Needed to Manage Risks* for defense acquisitions that should provide great guidance even for commercial enterprises (tinyurl.com/7kq6a98).

- **Service Availability.** Cloud providers need to reassure customers that they'll have regular and predictable access to their data and applications. For the IT teams, this implies an ability to scale-up as demand rises and scale-down as it subsides to produce an elastic computer resource that's cost effective.

- **Application Security.** Cloud providers ensure that applications available as a service via the cloud are secured by implementing testing and acceptance procedures for outsourced or packaged application code. They also require that application-security measures (application-level firewall and database auditing) be in place in the production environment (tinyurl.com/dbobvb).

- **Elastic Computing.** Elasticity is the "true golden nugget of cloud computing and what makes the entire concept extraordinarily evolutionary, if not revolutionary," says Dustin Owens, in the June 2010 issue of the <u>Communications of the ACM</u>. The National Institute of Standards and Technology (NIST) captures this important characteristic in its definition of cloud computing:

"Cloud computing is a model for enabling convenient, on-demand network access to a shared pool of configurable computing resources (e.g., networks, servers, storage, applications, and services) that can be rapidly provisioned and released with minimal management effort or service provider interaction."

- **Management**. Newer versions of management tools can bridge the gap between applications and data that are shared between local and cloud resources. This capability is only effective when it can range from the enterprise to the cloud. For example, System Center Configuration Manager will support "multiple device types" and let users "seamlessly access their data from virtually anywhere, across multiple device types while providing IT with unified management tools and centralized control," according to a recent post on the System Center team blog (tinyurl.com/29mtq4c).

- **Privacy**. Finally, providers ensure that all critical data (credit card numbers, for example) is masked and that only authorized users have access to data in its entirety. Moreover, digital identities and credentials must be protected—as should any data that the provider collects or produces about customer activity in the cloud.

4.4 Private Clouds

Many governments have enacted laws, regulations and certification programs aimed at protecting their citizens' privacy and their national interests. The result has been limited use of publicly available clouds for many applications that handle data that's protected by regulation.

For example, certifications of national bodies like the Federal Information Security Management Act, or FISMA, implementation project run by NIST will need to be considered in addition to other compliance requirements (tinyurl.com/yekw6ak). In response, some cloud services providers are creating clouds dedicated to use by U.S. federal agencies or other governmental bodies to make compliance checking easier.

With the snowstorms during winter 2010, even the U.S. federal government found itself shut down in Washington, DC. Suddenly, the idea of continued operation of government services from home or remote sites is no longer unthinkable. The risk of release of large quantities of private information acts as a counterweight to hold back exposing more data to the Internet at a time when the current trend is to limit the federal government's exposure.

As another example, local governments like the city of Newark, N.J., have more freedom to find cost-effective solutions that don't require heavy capital expenditures to make city employees more productive with a common set of tools and easy collaboration. "In the City of Newark, we're focused on ensuring that our IT modernization and cost-saving programs exceed the mayor's overall objectives of renewing government," says Michael Greene, CIO of the city of Newark (tinyurl.com/88alprj).

A number of independent software vendors have chosen to make their offerings available on cloud platforms like Windows Azure (tinyurl.com/7dkfpas). This already provides credibility with government agencies. Now, the Windows Azure cloud has become an application

---

HUMAN RESOURCES AND THE CLOUD

Cloud computing is making the fundamental responsibilities of the CIO even harder to accomplish, and hence the role is more important than ever to the enterprise. Two of those responsibilities are strategic investment in IT and the protection of the business from certain types of risk. To the first point, the commodity pricing of computing and storage, along with the opportunities presented by efficient scale up and scale down, are all factors that the CIO can't ignore when it comes to making big purchasing and technology adoption decisions. The challenge is that cloud platforms are still relatively immature, and hence there are hidden costs.

To the second point – managing risk – control of sensitive data is the main unsolved problem in cloud computing right now. For example, should the organization be storing strategic plans on a SharePoint site hosted in a data center that they don't own? Who else has access to that datacenter? What about data subject to Federal regulation? The savvy CIO realizes that he or she is in a unique position to understand the business needs, analyze the on- and off-premise solutions available, and engage with vendors to ensure that the proper balance of risk and cost is met.

Effectively managing cloud security requires buy-in from the entire IT organization. This is already having an effect on hiring decisions and has resulted in the creation of a new role: a DevOp, someone whose responsibilities blur the lines between software development and IT operations.

Any developer who's worked at a start-up already has a sense of what that entails. Those overlapping responsibilities are becoming more formalized. Indeed, if you're adopting cloud computing for any line of business applications, then your developers and operations people are already performing overlapping tasks.

platform that benefits both the developer community and governmental

HUMAN RESOURCES AND THE CLOUD (CONTINUED)

Looking for software developers to help you transition your IT projects into the cloud? The main thing to keep in mind about cloud computing is that it's still the early days. The typical experienced web application developer will eventually figure things out, but the organization that hires her needs to realize that hardly anybody has this particular combination of experience yet.

For example, with Amazon's EC2 service, she'll need to create and manage her own machine instances, understand the difference between blob and relational storage architectures, manage data backups, deal with load balancing, and consider the cost model and her budget. Or she'll need to coordinate with her IT operations people to do some or all of that stuff (and it'll all be new to them, too). But has she ever had to work that closely with IT operations people before? And since the IT people won't own the machines (Amazon does), do they even want to support this project?

All of those considerations have software architecture implications as well, so it's not like she can just merrily write code while the IT people go off and design the system. To continue the EC2 example, it has its own message passing and storage interfaces, so much of her code is going to be purpose built. And new code means bugs – has she developed the debugging skills necessary to triage an offsite system in a timely manner? The latter can be a real concern under a deadline, since many developers (and not just web developers) have never really been forced to learn how to debug. Microsoft's Azure cloud service presents similar challenges: understanding the storage options, message passing, debugging, and cost model, figuring out the split of responsibilities between operations and dev, and then architecting the application accordingly. None of these tasks is insurmountable, and all of the cloud vendors have case studies showing customers of various sizes using their services at scale. Although, it bears mentioning that those case study customers may have had invaluable internal assistance from the vendor.

One additional piece of guidance: do not hire that brilliant developer from outside and expect her to ramp-up on cloud computing, the existing service/technology, and the internal politics of the company at the same time. Instead, task the most senior internal developer with leading the transition, and fill in staff to support him or her as

4.5 Importance of Control

The AWS Storage Gateway (tinyurl.com/88p2fh9) is offered as an on-premises virtual machine image to which the customer attaches its own storage arrays. Data written via iSCSI to the on-premises gateway is then automatically replicated up to the Amazon cloud. In the cloud, it acts as a secondary copy in case the on-premises storage fails, and of course the cloud copy is accessible to cloud-based applications as well. It's a smart model.

What about security? As usual, the devil is in the details. Some of the details are documented on the AWS site (tinyurl.com/869ztb5). Commendably, during replication, the data traverses an encrypted tunnel (SSL). As well, when the data is received by Amazon's storage gateway proxy in the cloud, it's encrypted before it's written to permanent storage.

However, since Amazon has access to the encryption keys, that protection buys you checkbox compliance, but not much more. After all, whoever has access to the keys can decrypt the data, and that includes rogue system administrators, or even Amazon itself if under duress (subpoena, national security, etc.).

If the data is subject to regulation that says it must be encrypted, this feature probably meets that bar. However, if the data has value or sensitivity above and beyond that, a different approach is required.

One option is to ensure that the data written to the on-premises storage device is already encrypted. That can be accomplished by placing an encrypting proxy between the device and the on-premises data center. Data read through the proxy will be decrypted, while data propagated up to the cloud will remain encrypted (and then be encrypted again in the cloud, but that's okay).

One example of such a proxy is SecurEntity, a software library available from JW Secure (tinyurl.com/8xs869r).

4.6 Auditing and Access Control

Systems with robust auditing and access control do exist, although they're not widely deployed. For example, Microsoft has developed U-Prove (tinyurl.com/34hs7ol). Google also done research in this space – see their paper entitled "Selective Disclosure Credential Sets" (tinyurl.com/72u4yjn). (This paper is very technical and discusses the fun cryptography required to make such systems possible). Wikipedia's **digital identity** page also discusses selective disclosure in this context (tinyurl.com/6m2bgm).

NATIONAL STRATEGY FOR TRUSTED IDENTITIES IN CYBERSPACE

NSTIC is an initiative by NIST intended to coordinate with the private sector in an effort to standardize the protection of user identities online (http://tinyurl.com/8x3dwqs).

In order to be successful, a big part of that mission will have to be the creation and adoption of identity systems which offer two key features:

- When authenticating (i.e. logging on) to a website or service, users must be able to choose which details of their identity are disclosed. An example of this is buying liquor: when you show your driver's license in order to establish that you're over 21, you're also disclosing your address, your full name, and the fact that you have a driver's license, all of which are extraneous information for that transaction.

- The system must be resistant to collusion which can lead to privacy violation. For example, if I log onto a health website for cancer patients using my Facebook ID, Facebook knows it. However, as an identity provider, why should Facebook be told that I have cancer?

---

5 COMPLIANCE

5.1 Compliance in the Cloud

Establishing secure access is a logical first step to extending the enterprise into the cloud. By setting policies for compliance, reporting and remote connectivity now, you set the stage for how your team will work within the cloud in a smooth and secure fashion. Using Network Access Protection (NAP) with IPsec connectivity technologies like DirectAccess can help by improving your auditing and compliance reporting.

It can be difficult to identify and gather the necessary data when creating an auditing and reporting solution for a new DirectAccess or IPsec deployment. We will show in this chapter how a hypothetical company might create a DirectAccess and NAP solution. The design will provide reporting data to determine who was connected, when they were connected, and if the client computer was within compliance.

5.1.1   The Compliance Problem

As the workforce becomes increasingly mobile, more organizations are adopting flexible remote access technologies like DirectAccess. With DirectAccess, whenever an authorized machine connects to the Internet, the user is automatically connected to the remote network. Because remote clients can sometimes be out-of-date with security patches and possibly infected by malware, many organizations also deploy NAP with IPsec to help ensure that only healthy clients can access secured resources.

In industries like financial services, healthcare, and government, the importance of verifying that only healthy and approved clients connect to cloud-based or on-site network resources is essential for data integrity. These industries are often required by internal compliance policies and Federal law to confirm that there has been no access to PII, such as bank account numbers, names, and health records, by any unauthorized parties (including malware and unknown third-party applications).

As users seek easier remote access to their work resources, IT managers in these secure industries must also ensure that only healthy clients access the corporate network. Unfortunately, there are challenges to creating meaningful reports from NAP and DirectAccess logs.

Setting up a DirectAccess infrastructure for seamless remote client access, securing intranet resources with NAP and IPsec, and monitoring the policy through reporting is the solution. TechNet includes some good information about how to implement NAP with DirectAccess, but there's little guidance on how to effectively log and report on client health. For this chapter, we will examine a hypothetical company (Woodgrove National Bank) and show how a consultant could use some simple code and SQL queries to create human-readable reports that detail the clients that connected during a specified period of time and whether they were NAP-compliant.

5.1.2   Setting up NAP on Top of DirectAccess

DirectAccess requires that the connecting clients run a compatible version of Windows (Windows 7 Ultimate or Windows 7 Enterprise). These clients connect to a DirectAccess server running Windows Server 2008 R2. A DirectAccess deployment can include one or more DirectAccess servers. (We recommend at least two servers to help load balance on busy networks.) The deployment also must include a network location server (to determine whether the client is connected to the Internet or intranet) and one or more certification revocation list (CRL) distribution points (used to track clients that should no longer be allowed access). To learn how to design a DirectAccess deployment, see the DirectAccess Design Guide on TechNet (tinyurl.com/72hr9z6).

When adding NAP on top of DirectAccess, you must implement the IPsec enforcement method for NAP. When using IPsec, clients that are NAP-compliant are granted health certificates. If a computer is not compliant, it's not allowed to communicate with computers that are compliant. To learn about how to design and deploy NAP, see Planning DirectAccess with Network Access Protection on TechNet (tinyurl.com/7crkr8h). To learn about how to design NAP with IPsec as the enforcement method, see IPsec Enforcement Design on TechNet (tinyurl.com/77cy62j).

It's interesting to consider how the NAP IPsec enforcement scenario works within the context of DirectAccess and its IPsec connection policies. First, because DirectAccess uses IPsec for authentication and confidentiality, the NAP enforcement scenario in a DirectAccess deployment must be IPsec. Second, keep in mind that the AuthIP component of IPsec lets you configure two separate authentication requirements in the policy, such that the connection must meet both to succeed. Typically, if both AuthIP authentication options are configured, the first is the machine credential and the second is the user credential. However, it is technically possible to configure two machine credentials.

Where does NAP fit into the AuthIP policies? The NAP/IPsec enforcement scenario gives healthy machines a certificate with the health object identifier (OID). The AuthIP policy engine includes an option for requiring that health OID. Thus, only healthy machines will be able to meet the first AuthIP authentication requirement and establish an IPsec connection to the DirectAccess server.

Finally, the user credential is the purpose of the second AuthIP authentication option. Technically, the user credential is optional for DirectAccess. In other words, clients could authenticate to the DirectAccess endpoint using just a machine certificate. Security-conscious IT personnel should be nervous about giving full remote network access without strong authentication. At the minimum, therefore, the AuthIP policy should be configured to require a second authentication of Kerberos. Requiring a certificate for the user credential, as in the Woodgrove National Bank scenario, is preferable because it reduces the risk of remote static password attacks.

In this scenario, the network security and compliance departments of Woodgrove National Bank have requested a report showing who has connected to the corporate network over a specified period of time and whether or not those clients were NAP-compliant. These groups believe that there may have been a compromise of customer data during that time. As a consultant for the bank, we need to determine how to enable after-the-fact reporting for DirectAccess and NAP, and then pull that information into a human-readable report.

5.1.3   Proper Policy Configuration

In this hypothetical scenario, Woodgrove National Bank has configured DirectAccess so the IPsec policy requires client certificates that include the NAP system health OID and the client authentication OID. Woodgrove is using NAP in enforcement mode (rather than just reporting mode), which means unhealthy clients will be blocked from communicating with healthy clients.

Finally, Woodgrove has configured the DirectAccess IPsec policy to use two certificate-based credentials—one from the client computer and one from the user. As previously suggested, Woodgrove chose the double-certificate configuration in order to better utilize its PKI investment, to eliminate static passwords for remote access and to take advantage of certificate auto-enrollment.

The remainder of this story assumes that you have a working knowledge of how DirectAccess, NAP and the IPsec enforcement mode work. Please see the following resources to learn more about these technologies:

- DirectAccess Executive Overview (tinyurl.com/7tm4xea)

- Introduction to Network Access Protection (tinyurl.com/6msz68u)

- Understanding NAP IPsec Enforcement (tinyurl.com/7hejr6s)

The following reporting solution takes advantage of the built-in auditing features of IPsec on the DirectAccess server as well as the auditing capabilities of the Health Registration Authority (HRA) feature of the Network Policy Server (NPS). These auditing features produce events in the system and security event logs, which we extract and report. In developing this approach, we found that the HRA events are produced by default, while the IPsec events might have to be explicitly enabled. You can use the following commands at a command prompt window to enable the IPsec events:

```
auditpol.exe /set /category:"Logon/Logoff"
/subcategory:"IPsec Main Mode" /success:enable
/failure:enable

auditpol.exe /set /category:"Logon/Logoff"
/subcategory:"IPsec Quick Mode" /success:enable
/failure:enable

auditpol.exe /set /category:"Logon/Logoff"
/subcategory:"IPsec Extended Mode" /success:enable
/failure:enable
```

5.1.4   DirectAccess Health Reporting

To begin working with the NAP and DirectAccess events from Woodgrove National Bank, we downloaded and installed Log Parser 2.2 from Microsoft (tinyurl.com/8xp4z5a). Log Parser is an indispensable tool for a project like this, where you must explore a new event source and develop an appropriate schema. In summary, Log Parser can import from and export to several data formats, including the Windows event log (.evtx), CSV, and SQL.

The next step is to capture the events that are of interest. Those include:

- IPsec security association-related events in the security log of the DirectAccess servers.

- Health Registration Authority-related events in the security and system logs of the HRA server, or servers (this item only applies if you're using NAP).

An ideal solution for gathering those events is both automated and centralized. The Windows event forwarding feature is one option. Microsoft System Center would be more typical in a large production deployment. In our case, we did not want to introduce new dependencies for production servers, so we used simple scripts for gathering the events.

Given that approach, the challenge is twofold. First, because the goal is to correlate multiple data sources, it's important that the data from all of the sources be gathered roughly at the same time. Second, because we're only taking a snapshot of the logs, and high-traffic event logs roll over quickly, it's inevitable that some correlating events will be missing, especially at the edge of the time period of the snapshot. This does not invalidate the experiment, but it does make it more difficult to tune the queries.

For each IPsec main-mode security association (on one of the DirectAccess servers) we expect to see NAP health traffic (on one of the HRA servers). In NAP reporting mode, the client machine may have been compliant or not. In NAP enforcement mode, the client machine should have been compliant. Otherwise, how does it have a valid certificate for authenticating to the DirectAccess server and establishing a security association (SA)? Suppose we do a one-time log capture on all

DirectAccess and HRA servers simultaneously at 3 p.m. It's possible we would see the main mode security association (MM SA) event, but not the health event.

Even more likely is that we would see IPsec quick mode security association (QM SA) and IPsec extended mode security association (EM SA) events, but not the MM SA or health events. The former can occur as much as an hour or more after the latter. In addition, because the logs on separate servers almost certainly rollover at different frequencies, we might have events from 2 p.m. on the DirectAccess server, but events only as early as 2:30 p.m. on the HRA. For these reasons, we want to reiterate that it's important to use centralized event gathering in production.

5.1.5   Generating the Data

To generate the data, we ran scripts on the DirectAccess servers and the HRA servers. We also configured the scripts to be run automatically with Task Scheduler. We configured the script to run on the DirectAccess server and all of the HRAs one time, simultaneously.

Collecting Data on DirectAccess Servers

We used the following script to capture events on the DirectAccess server (see **Table 1**).

```
set MPATH=c:\temp\Logs

%MPATH%\LogParser.exe "SELECT * INTO
%MPATH%\DA_Security_Events_%COMPUTERNAME%.csv FROM
Security WHERE EventCategory=12549 OR
EventCategory=12547 OR EventCategory=12550" -o:CSV
```

> **NOTE**
>
> This script uses a local copy of LogParser.exe (and LogParser.dll, its dependency). This reference was used for convenience so that we could easily copy the script from server to server.

The following table details the events that were captured from the DirectAccess server using a script run automatically with Task Scheduler.

Table 1 - Details of the events captured from the DirectAccess server

Event	Description
12547	IPsec Main Mode Security Association information
12549	IPsec Quick Mode Security Association information
12550	IPsec Extended Mode Security Association information

Collecting Data on the HRA Servers

To capture events on the HRA servers, we used the following script.

```
set MPATH=c:\temp\Logs

%MPATH%\LogParser.exe "SELECT * INTO
%MPATH%\HRA_Security_Events_%COMPUTERNAME%.csv FROM
Security WHERE EventCategory=12552" -o:CSV

%MPATH%\LogParser.exe "SELECT * INTO
%MPATH%\HRA_System_Events_%COMPUTERNAME%.csv FROM
System WHERE SourceName='HRA'" -o:CSV
```

NOTE

In the HRA script, event category 12552 maps to the Network Policy
Server service.

5.1.6 Importing the Data

After the scripts had run, we gathered the output CSV files to a separate
machine running SQL Server 2008. We used the following script to
import the CSV data into SQL.

```
LogParser.exe "SELECT * INTO DaSasTable FROM DA_*.csv"
-i:CSV -o:SQL -server:dev1 -database:NapDa -
createTable:ON -maxStrFieldLen:1023

LogParser.exe "SELECT * INTO HraSecurityEventsTable
FROM HRA_Security_*.csv" -i:CSV -o:SQL -server:dev1 -
database:NapDa -createTable:ON -maxStrFieldLen:1023

LogParser.exe "SELECT * INTO HraSystemEventsTable  FROM
HRA_System_*.csv" -i:CSV -o:SQL -server:dev1 -
database:NapDa -createTable:ON -maxStrFieldLen:1023
```

NOTES

- The name of the SQL host machine is **dev1**. The database is named **NapDa**, and the database was created using the default values in SQL Management Studio.

- The three tables, **DaSasTable**, **HraSecurityEventsTable**, and **HraSystemEventsTable** did not already exist. The -createTable:ONLog Parser command-line option specifies Log Parser to automatically create those tables with a suitable schema based on the input data (the event log CSV files, in this case).

- The **-maxStrFieldLen:1023** setting is important in this scenario. Without this setting, a default varchar field length of 255 would be used by Log Parser for the various event log string fields. However, the event log CSV format has some data strings that are longer than that (particularly in the Strings field; see **Figure 6**), and it's important that they not be truncated. Experimentally, a default length of 1023 seems to be adequate.

The following figure shows the schema that resulted from the Log Parser CSV event log import.

Figure 6 – Schema for the Log Parser CSV event log import

DaSasTable

Column Name	Data Type	Allow Nulls
Filename	varchar(1023)	☑
RowNumber	int	☑
EventLog	varchar(1023)	☑
RecordNumber	int	☑
TimeGenerated	datetime	☑
TimeWritten	datetime	☑
EventID	int	☑
EventType	int	☑
EventTypeName	varchar(1023)	☑
EventCategory	int	☑
EventCategoryName	varchar(1023)	☑
SourceName	varchar(1023)	☑
Strings	varchar(1023)	☑
ComputerName	varchar(1023)	☑
SID	varchar(1023)	☑
Message	varchar(1023)	☑
Data	varchar(1023)	☑
		☐

5.1.7   Preparing the Data

In creating the DirectAccess health report, the primary challenge with extracting the required data is working with the event log CSV format based on data strings. In the context of a graphical user interface (GUI), the data are interleaved into static strings that describe the meaning of each data field. The data strings include everything interesting to a DirectAccess health report, including user names, machine names, policy group names, and IP addresses.

The data strings are concatenated into a single CSV field, and eventually a single SQL column (again, strings). Each string is separated from the next with a "|" character. One option would be to tokenize the strings, before or immediately after importing the data into SQL. However, our preference was to instead parse the strings after they're in SQL, then to extract the few specific data items we needed and populate separate SQL tables with those items.

Accomplishing this task with string pattern matching with T-SQL is difficult. As an alternative, we used an approach documented in a previous *MSDN Magazine* article, "Regular Expressions Make Pattern Matching and Data Extraction Easier" — implementing user-defined functions for SQL using C#, specifically for the purpose of regular expression-based pattern matching (tinyurl.com/5fzmh5).

Using Visual Studio 2008, we followed the steps in that article almost exactly, although it was helpful to refer to additional documentation on getting initial SQL and CLR integration working with Visual Studio (tinyurl.com/6meenat). Also, because of the inherent complexity of regular expressions (RegEx), it was helpful to refer to the documentation for that technology as well, particularly the section on grouping, as that's the approach used by the sample code from the *MSDN Magazine* article (http://tinyurl.com/7op847b).

The following code sample details the source code for the SQL user-defined function that exposes RegEx capabilities into our SELECT statements. The function is called RegexGroup, just like the one from the article. We made one modification in the first two lines of the function body so that we can check for NULL input values. Before we added these two lines, we encountered numerous exceptions because several of our SQL helper table columns (described here) have NULL values.

51

```
usingSystem;

usingSystem.Data;

usingSystem.Data.SqlClient;

usingSystem.Data.SqlTypes;

usingMicrosoft.SqlServer.Server;

usingSystem.Text.RegularExpressions;

publicpartialclassUserDefinedFunctions

{

    [Microsoft.SqlServer.Server.SqlFunction]

publicstaticSqlChars RegexGroup(

SqlChars input, SqlString pattern, SqlString name)

{

if (true == input.IsNull)

returnSqlChars.Null;

Regex regex = newRegex(pattern.Value, Options);

Match match = regex.Match(newstring(input.Value));

returnmatch.Success ?

newSqlChars(match.Groups[name.Value].Value) :
SqlChars.Null;

}

};
```

The following SQL commands create and populate two helper tables consisting of strings extracted from the initial data set using RegEx.

```
/* Create the User-Computer-Address mapping helper
table */

/* This step should only be performed once per data
set */

CREATE TABLE UserComputerAndAddr
```

```
(

[RowN] int null,

[UserName] varchar(1023) null,

[ComputerName] varchar(1023) null,

[Address] varchar(1023) null

)


/* Populate the User-Computer-Address table */

/* This step should only be performed once per data
set */

INSERT INTO UserComputerAndAddr(RowN, UserName,
ComputerName, Address)

SELECT RowNumber,

  dbo.RegexGroup([Strings],N'(?<un>[0-9a-zA-
Z]+)@redmond.corp.microsoft.com',N'un'),

  dbo.RegexGroup([Strings],N'(?<machine>[0-9a-zA-Z\-
]+)(?<!CO1RED-TPM-
01)\$@redmond.corp.microsoft.com',N'machine'),

  dbo.RegexGroup([Strings],N'(?<ipv6addr>[0-9a-fA-
F]{1,4}:[0-9a-fA-F]{1,4}:[0-9a-fA-F]{1,4}:[0-9a-fA-
F]{1,4}:[0-9a-fA-F]{1,4}:[0-9a-fA-F]{1,4}:[0-9a-fA-
F]{1,4}:[0-9a-fA-F]{1,4})',N'ipv6addr')

FROM [NapDa].[dbo].[DaSasTable]


/* Create the Computer-Health mapping helper table */

/* This step should only be performed once per data
set */

CREATE TABLE ComputerHealth

(

[RowN] int null,

[TimeGenerated] datetime null,
```

```
[EventType] int null,

[ComputerName] varchar(1023) null

)



/* Populate the Computer-Health mapping table */

/* This step should only be performed once per data
set */

INSERT INTO ComputerHealth(RowN, TimeGenerated,
EventType, ComputerName)

SELECT RowNumber,

  TimeGenerated,

  EventType,

  dbo.RegexGroup([Strings],N'REDMOND\\(?<machine>[0-
9a-zA-Z\-]+)\$',N'machine')

FROM [NapDa].[dbo].[HraSystemEventsTable]
```

You can get a sense of the string patterns by examining the first SELECT statement and its use of the RegexGroup function installed with the technique that we described. **Table 2** details the three RegEx patterns that we defined.

Table 2 – The three RegEx patterns defined by using SQL commands

RegEx Pattern	Notes
User name	Example: ichiro@redmond.corp.microsoft.com
Computer name	Example: dan-dev-1@redmond.corp.microsoft.com Notice that we are explicitly excluding matches against the DirectAccess server itself in this pattern.
IPv6 address	Example: 2001:0:4137:1f6b:8c8:2f30:e7ed:73a8 • This pattern will not match all valid IPv6 addresses. You will need to enhance this pattern if you want to use it in other contexts. • While there are other embedded IPv6 address fields

	in the Strings column, the client address seemed to be the only one matching this pattern. You might need to revisit this if you get unexpected addresses in your queries.

Together, those regular expressions help to create a table, which consists of the User, Computer, and Address information from each row in the **DaSasTable** (i.e., the IPsec SA events exported from the DirectAccess machine).

After the **UserComputerAndAddr** table is created and populated, a second table is created that maps computer name to event type for each row in the **HraSystemEventsTable** table. If you examine the computer name pattern, you will see that the computer name format is different in this log from the DirectAccess log. In this case, we are looking for strings like REDMOND\dan-dev-1. **Table 3** details the different events that might be present in the **EventType** field.

Table 3 - Event types that might be present in the EventType field

Event Type	Description
0	Success. The computer submitted a compliant NAP statement of health.
1	Failure. The computer was non-compliant with the NAP policy.

In the health report for this deployment, we only expect to see event type 0. That's because NAP is being used in enforcement mode. As you will see below, we are also filtering on successful IPsec security associations. If the client was non-compliant, it should not have been able to acquire a valid IPsec certificate and establish an SA. On the other hand, if your organization has deployed NAP in reporting mode, you will expect to see some non-compliant machines connected. The relative percentage of compliant versus non-compliant machines connected to the network is an important statistic to report.

> **NOTE**
>
> When using tables for RegEx results, we recommend that you use

> permanent SQL tables. If you use temporary tables (as we do for the demo in the next step), the RegEx queries will be slow.

5.1.8   Building the Report

With the regular expression parsing complete and the helper tables created, we can now focus on building the health report itself. Once the data has been prepared, writing the report queries is relatively easy.

The purpose of this sample report is to list all users who established a DirectAccess connection between 3 p.m. and 4 p.m. on May 5, 2010. Along with the user name, the report lists the computer name and health status.

In order to identify those users, we will start by querying for successful (event type 8) QM SAs (event category 12549) within that period. The QM SA event is useful in this scenario because IPsec has been configured to require second-factor authentication (the user's credentials). We chose to use this reporting approach because QM SAs are relatively short-lived (an hour, in this case, with an inactivity timeout of five minutes) and hence are useful for auditing access. An MM SA, in contrast, only implies the use of the computer credential and persists for eight hours by default (although we recommend decreasing the MM lifespan if auditing is an important component of your DirectAccess deployment).

Unfortunately, the QM events do not include either the user name or machine name; they only include the IP address. To map the IP address to a machine name and user name, we can use a few SELECT statements in our SQL query. The first SELECT statement in the following query will return the list of addresses that appear in new QM SAs within that period. The second SELECT statement uses those addresses to map to the user name and computer name that are associated with that address elsewhere in the log. (This user/computer/address association is in the EM SA events. These events are critical for this exercise because they contain all three values; if you're not requiring IPsec second-authentication, then you will not be able to do this type of reporting.)

```
/* The following steps build the report, based on the
three imported tables

* plus the two helpers above. These steps can be run
```

```
any number of times as

* you refine your query.

*/

/* Create a temporary table to populate as the final
report */

CREATE TABLE #SaHealthReport

(

[UserName] varchar(1023) null,

[ComputerName] varchar(1023) null,

[HealthEventType] int null

)


/* Run a query to find all IPsec Quick Mode Security
Associations established

* within a given period. Populate a temporary table
with the client IPv6

* addresses. */

SELECT DISTINCT[Address] INTO #TempAddresses

FROM [NapDa].[dbo].[DaSasTable] JOIN
[NapDa].[dbo].[UserComputerAndAddr]

     ON RowN = RowNumber

WHERE [EventType]=8 AND

     [EventCategory]=12549 AND

     ([TimeGenerated] BETWEEN'2010-05-10
15:00:00.000' AND '2010-05-10 16:00:00.000')


/* Map the QM SA addresses to user and computer names
and insert those into

* the final report. */

INSERT INTO #SaHealthReport(UserName,ComputerName)
```

```
SELECT
UserComputerAndAddr.UserName,UserComputerAndAddr.Compu
terName

FROM [NapDa].[dbo].[UserComputerAndAddr] JOIN
#TempAddresses

      ON #TempAddresses.Address =
UserComputerAndAddr.Address

WHERE (UserComputerAndAddr.UserName IS NOT NULL) AND
(UserComputerAndAddr.ComputerName IS NOT NULL)


/* Populate the health column of the report. */

UPDATE #SaHealthReport

SET HealthEventType = ComputerHealth.EventType

FROM #SaHealthReport JOIN
[NapDa].[dbo].[ComputerHealth]

      ON #SaHealthReport.ComputerName =
ComputerHealth.ComputerName


/* Display all rows and columns of the report. */

SELECT DISTINCT *

FROM #SaHealthReport
```

The final step in populating the SaHealthReport report table is to correlate the HRA health information with the computer and user identity information, which has thus far come exclusively from the DirectAccess server. The incorporation of the HRA server information into this mix is a powerful tool that allows you to determine whether the computers connecting remotely to your network are introducing risk (due to non-compliance). See the UPDATE statement in the previous SQL query—the correlation between DirectAccess and HRA data is accomplished by using the client computer name.

The following table shows sample data that could be returned from a completed health report.

Table 4 - Sample completed health report

UserName	ComputerName	HealthEventType
Ichiro	ichiroadmin1	0
Grinch	whoville-cli	0
Raquel	omybc	0

You can establish reporting on IPsec (including DirectAccess) and NAP deployment relatively easily with some custom scripts and the Log Parser tool. This approach will help a company start to create a secure framework for exposing line-of-business services, whether on-site or in the cloud.

5.2 Insider Threats

Two recent high-profile news stories served as a reminder of the tough challenges faced by IT managers, specifically regarding insider threats. That is, the potential damage that can be caused, intentionally or unintentionally, by people with privileged access to data and systems.

The first insider threat story of note is WikiLeaks (tinyurl.com/2ft8pf5). At first blush, the type of threat represented by WikiLeaks is this: people can take sensitive information from inside an organization, publish it to a forum designed for that purpose, and make a big splash. But more generally, the threat is of any sort of unauthorized disclosure (e.g. classified data; software source code; a customer list; etc.), and it's important to note that it can happen maliciously or accidentally.

Mitigation of the unauthorized disclosure risk can be a major effort. Organizations must undertake the time-consuming and frequently ambiguous process of:

- Locating and classifying data.
- Determining who has access to that data, who should have access, and how and when they should have access.
- Instituting the necessary access controls for enforcement.
- Auditing access and archiving logs.

Even so, discretionary access controls don't protect the organization against rogue insiders who are authorized to access certain information but not to disclose it externally. Some additional protection is afforded by commercial Data Loss Prevention (DLP) technologies, but it is infeasible to guard against every possible way that sensitive data can be exfiltrated or disclosed (tinyurl.com/ygkyjld). The importance of the human element – including instituting periodic vetting of personnel in a manner commensurate with the risk – cannot be overlooked, and neither can the importance of being prepared in advance to respond to a disclosure incident when one occurs.

The second prominent insider threat story is StuxNet (tinyurl.com/2vol5nk). StuxNet makes an interesting contrast to the WikiLeaks story for two reasons. First, it reinforces the point that the insider can be innocent, albeit careless. While it's admittedly unclear to what extent user carelessness played a role in the propagation of StuxNet, the takeaway for the rest of us is clear: a trusted user can, for example, introduce an infected USB key into the vulnerable internal LAN. User education is crucial.

But StuxNet also reminds us of the importance of two parallel efforts: secure configuration on the part of the IT organization and the disciplined employment of Security Development Lifecycle practices on the part of software vendors.

6 CLOUD PLATFORMS

6.1 Various Cloud Platforms

There are generally two different types of virtualization, specifically as they pertain to cloud computing. The first, infrastructure virtualization, is what Amazon offers with its Elastic Compute Cloud—known as EC2; for a more detailed introduction, see the EC2 article on Wikipedia (tinyurl.com/5edaqk). The key point is that, at first blush, infrastructure virtualization feels like an easy transition from onsite servers to cloud computing, because it gives you the ability to remotely manage your own servers in cloud in much the same way that you manage them in an onsite datacenter (for example, via RDP or SSH).

However, like any technology transition, infrastructure virtualization places a burden on IT staff to develop new tooling and management scripts. That's because the underlying virtual fabric is different from what was being used before (for example, ESX or bare metal). The second type of virtualization we want to highlight is application runtime virtualization. This is the model used by Windows Azure and the Google App Engine. This approach places a different kind of burden on the IT staff because it's difficult to control, regulate, and monitor. There are two challenges, both of which we'll return to later in this chapter:

- LOB developers can deploy apps directly to the cloud without going through IT approval processes.

- Virtualized storage provided in the cloud may not comply with IT controls such as data loss prevention, access and auditing policies, encryption, and sovereignty—we have written about the latter in the previous issue of the JW Secure Informer newsletter (tinyurl.com/6usj25s).

Despite the challenges, it's important to note that application virtualization in the cloud is a boon for developers and software start-ups for many of the same reasons that it's painful to IT. From a cost perspective, cloud computing is proving to be irresistible to larger businesses because it facilitates the current trend of transforming capital expenses, such as in-house servers, into operational expenses, such as a monthly cloud services bill.

Plus, once developers have been trained on the new cloud computing environment, the result may be an overall reduction in the cost of LOB app deployment and lifecycle management. And let's not forget the inherent scalability benefits of cloud computing.

The major tech vendors recognize this, of course, and are doing everything they can to entice LOB developers to use their cloud platforms. Tight integration with the developer tool chain is the key.

On August 31, 2011, VMware announced its competitive answer to Windows Azure: vFabric (tinyurl.com/776uq9t). The most notable quality of vFabric is its tight integration with the Java-based SpringSource Tool Suite, which includes a reputable runtime library and also offers tight integration with the Eclipse integrated development environment (IDE).

This is the same approach that Microsoft is using: deploying applications directly from the developer's desktop to the cloud is becoming easier with each new version of its Visual Studio IDE and the Azure integration tools.

Why does IDE integration matter? Because building a cloud computing platform is enormously expensive, and the only way companies like Microsoft and VMware/EMC stand a chance of making back their investment is to make it brain-dead simple for every developer in the world to run his or her app in the cloud. That means the lowest common denominator: write a Visual Basic app, click a button, it's running in the cloud and you're done – next project. No setup, no confusing configuration, no keys, etc.

Problem: The focus on this one-click-deployment strategy is convenient, but it leaves some unanswered questions in the security department.

6.2 Hybrid

If you believe even a fraction of the press about cloud computing, you want to understand not only how to harness its benefits for your own organization, but how do to that without losing control of information which is critical to the success of the organization.

Most early cloud implementations will be hybrids of services that run on-premises with services deployed in the cloud. This is the scenario that we'll explore so that you can begin a gradual move into the cloud without undue fear of the loss of control. You will learn how to control applications and services dynamically deployed from a variety of cloud environments into devices like user desktops, Microsoft Terminal Services, and a range of mobile devices.

The goal is to evolve from control of computers to control of services available to users. This takes existing service-oriented architecture (SOA) and machine virtualization to the next step. The result will be increased business productivity with less overhead, as the user will be able to work anywhere on any capable device without any worry about application deployment.

6.3 Two Ways to Look at Cloud Services

Let's just accept as given that your organization will soon have some cloud exposure, so it's important to plan the transition of some applications into the cloud. There are at least two distinct axes on which a cloud service can be measured.

Table 5 - Axis 1 Delivering services to three broad sizes of customer organization

Organization Size	Authentication	Collaboration	Typical Cloud Use
Small organization, up to 25 users	Workgroup	Individual	Applications like email
Medium organization up to 250 users	Domain	Federation	Platform, database, ERP
Enterprise class organization	Multiple domains	Dedicated	Load and location leveling

The details in the previous table are generalizations of the ways that organizations of different sizes approach the web. Small organizations and small departments within large organizations typically pick a complete software solution like email or office productivity applications. These solutions are isolated from the organization's other IT resources and offer fixed management control experiences that are a part of the total solution.

Once an organization gets to the size where they can fund a full time IT administrator they will look at more personalized cloud solutions where they have more control over the application. New projects can start completely in the cloud when they have no important dependencies on existing business data. Projects which involve extensions to existing on-premises applications will have greater dependency on on-premises servers and hence are more difficult to move into the cloud. Larger enterprises will take on even more flexibility by renting virtual images on machine managed by external or internal cloud providers.

In summary, while the small organization has little need or capability to manage their cloud deployments, each step beyond that will require management tools to control both on-premises and cloud resources, something that has been very difficult to accomplish up until now.

Table 6 - Axis 2 Delivering services at three broad depths of engagement (Service Models)

Offering	Type	Industry	Microsoft
SAAS: Application Software as a Service	Fixed apps like email, ERP, CRP	Salesforce	BPOS, Office 365, Windows InTune
PAAS: Platform as a Service	Controlled space for apps or Database	Google, Facebook	SQL Azure, Azure App Fabric
IAAS: Infrastructure as a Service	Complete access to dynamic VMs	Amazon AWS, Private Clouds	Windows Server Hyper-V

This axis is focused on the vendor product solutions rather than the customer needs like the first axis. Vendors must commoditize the service offering to keep costs low, so it is incumbent on the customer to assure that the SLA from the vendor will meet their performance expectations. At each step in the service offering, from software to platform and infrastructure, the customer assumes more and more of the management load in exchange for more and more flexibility in the service offering.

6.4 What's Your Motivation?

It is interesting to look at which companies are moving first to the cloud. The answer can be summed up in these two categories:

- **Who has the most to gain?** Any organization that is planning a switch away from an old or expensive platform will be highly incented by the reduced capital expenditure of the cloud. Any organization that has rapid growth or highly variable compute loads will find the flexibility of the cloud to scale both up and down to be a real cost advantage.

- **Who has the least to lose?** Generally the larger, more diverse enterprises have the most to lose and are the least likely to move, absent some major shift in their business model (like a divestiture). The smaller the company the smaller the existing investment and the less concern about moving to the cloud. According to research by McKinsey, SMBs with fewer than 250 employees are more than twice as likely as big enterprises to adopt cloud services. The evidence from BPOS deployments bears this out (tinyurl.com/7fkhwk7).

6.5 Management Control as a Service

A big problem created by hybrid clouds is that there is a duplicated set of IT controls: one on-premise in the enterprise Active Directory, and one in the cloud under a different namespace. That separation means that there is a synchronization problem between these broad deployment areas. All of these services need to be controlled by the customer.

That control function is sometimes described as a separate service which could also be run on-premises or in the cloud, but really it is just another application. Whether the control application is supplied by software as a service (SAAS), platform as a service (PAAS), infrastructure as a service (IAAS) or on-premises is not as important as determining a control architecture and solution management software that will work for the entire organization in a hybrid environment. After a solution is chosen, the location where that solution runs will be easier to determine.

One case where management has been deployed as a service is Microsoft InTune (tinyurl.com/3qut7xg). For a low monthly fee for each PC, it adds cloud management of the PC together with an upgrade subscription. Using the same anti-malware client code as Microsoft Security Essentials and Forefront Endpoint Protection it provides small to medium organizations with robust anti-malware protection to any location accessible to the Internet.

For hybrid clouds, it's important to note that management is a service that needs to be hosted somewhere with collectors in all of the locations where the cloud infrastructure is deployed.

Until recently management of the cloud meant management of the virtual machines that are the core infrastructure for the cloud. An example is System Center Virtual Machine Manager (SCVMM), which provides for centralized management of physical and virtual on-premises servers (tinyurl.com/6rqf3qv). But as more organizations deploy hybrid environments, the inability of existing tools to manage two disparate and often incompatible domains has become clear. **Figure 7** shows how the release of System Center 2012 suite addresses cloud management issues (http://tinyurl.com/7sawcm7).

Figure 7 - Managing multiple cloud sites

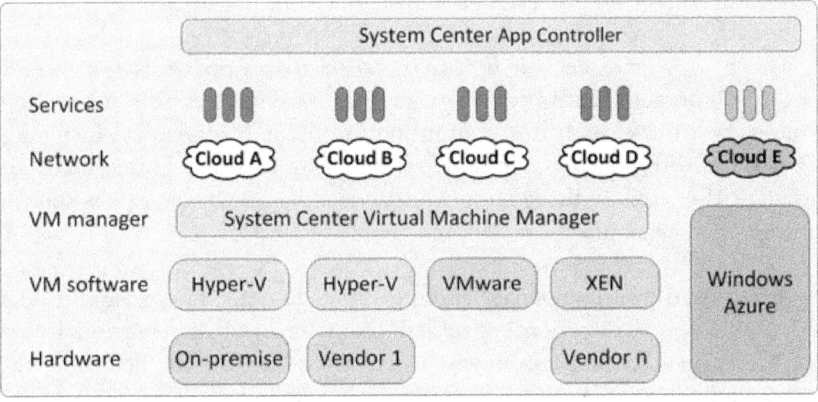

While SCVMM will be upgraded and continue to support individual cloud deployments, a new System Center product called App Controller (previously known under the code name Concero) will offer control of multiple cloud deployments, both private (on-premises) and public (Azure). The initial 2010 RTM release supports only public Azure and private deployments; however, other vendors are expected to take advantage of its extensibility. For example, Citrix has provided support for XEN virtual machines in App Controller.

This continues a process where the cloud provider shields the IT department from all concern about deploying and maintaining the hardware of servers and routers. The cloud IAAS can be assumed to exist, and IT staff should focus on providing applications and services to the organization.

6.6 User-Oriented Architecture

While the next generation of management tools is responding to the hybrid cloud trend, another important trend to address is the so-called bring–your-own-device (BYOD) trend– that is, users accessing corporate resources with personal hardware.

Again, the major management solutions are responding. For example, user-centric application delivery is enabled with SCCM 2012 and focuses on providing extreme mobility of a specific resource for a specific user. IT focus is moving from work-life balance to work-life integration. Users expected to be able to work anywhere, anytime so the solutions and their architectures need to be designed with that as a primary goal.

The SLA guarantees on up-time needed to support this must be at least 99.9 percent with better guarantees possible as the technology progresses. For on-premises computing the focus has been on insulating the service offerings from cloud outages, but as users increasingly are moving off-premises, there are fewer services that must operate when the Internet is unavailable.

It has been possible since Windows 2000 to offer fine-grained policy and application deployment, specified to the level of the individual user, but that capability has not been widely used because of licensing and device limitations. Device affinity is now available in SCCM 2010. If the user is not on one of their "primary devices" then the strategy is to provide them some other type of access like Terminal Services or Office 365.

Since not all devices have the same storage or other resources, application deployment options need to understand device capabilities. If the IT infrastructure is to provide user access to any document, anywhere, it needs to adapt to the device. For example, Windows Phone 7 comes with a version of Microsoft Office. So if the user is accessing a Word document from a smart phone, in some cases the Word document can be downloaded to the smart phone, but in other devices the document will need to be rendered on a web or terminal server to allow remote access to the document.

This is a different way of thinking about application deployment in which the industry is moving from managing the workstation to adapting to users and their devices. The implication is that commercially successful applications will need to be available for all common deployment mechanisms in order for management software to succeed in providing anywhere access.

6.7 Authentication of the Cloud Servers

Security breaches have taught us to ensure that both ends of any connection are well known. Microsoft Terminal Services added TLS (aka SChannel) protection to ensure that users were not spoofed by rogue servers masquerading as official sites, or creating a man-in-the-middle attack (tinyurl.com/fco32). These types of attacks are prevented by authentication of both ends of any connection.

Virtual private networks (VPN) have long been used as a gateway for securely accessing organizational assets. With DirectAccess available on Windows 7, there is now a way for local and remote computers to use IPSec to verify that each computer is part of the same security domain, as well as to provide "always on" management capability.

If users are not part of the same security domain, the best available solution is TLS with certificates issued to all machines (or users) that need to trust each other. Today, web servers can acquire enhanced validation (EV) certificates to use in TLS connections. Users can additionally be authenticated by smart cards as a part of TLS mutual authentication. However, the difficulty of deploying certificates and private keys to end users has caused most user authentication to fall back to user names and passwords for authentication.

6.8 Control of Data in the Cloud

There are two aspects to the control of data in the cloud. The first is whether the data should be placed in the cloud at all. If the data is moved to the cloud, the second control aspect is how to prevent it from leaving the cloud. The physical location of the data may be important when corporate or governmental compliance is a factor. The management control programs will need to be able track compliance with policy restrictions. Government, risk and compliance (GRC) papers and solutions have been collected by Microsoft on the System Center team blog (tinyurl.com/27ee4pv).

As we observed above, it is critical that IT take a proactive approach to setting policies for corporate data and cloud computing, otherwise some other business group at your organization may effectively make the decision for you. As one example of data creep, the need for data access authorization in the cloud carries with it the idea that some authorization claim will need to be presented to those cloud servers. Next we will consider the authentication of users and then the authorization of their access to cloud resources.

6.9 Single Sign-On

The advantage of having a single point of control over users' access to any organizational assets should be clear. Central control of user authentication credentials allows immediate and full revocation of access to all organizational assets when that user is no longer part of the organization. Central control also provides consistent policy for attributes like password strength.

Extending centralized authentication policy to cloud resources provides not only continuity of control but also maximizes user convenience so that the user need not provide different credentials based on the location of the resource. This will be particularly important as resources migrate to the cloud over time.

The history of Web SSO started in the middle 1990's and has not resulted in a widely acceptable solution as yet. The current successes are with a federated approach using the security assertion markup language (SAML) that assumes that a user is already well known in one namespace and needs to establish authorized access in another. A federated ID does not provide a broad web based solution that would accommodate all of the services currently under development for cloud based services.

OAuth 2.0 is a new protocol that extends the architecture of OAuth 1.0 to allow for selective disclosure of the type needed in a world where user privacy is mandated by so many government regulations (tinyurl.com/3yeubuf). Even though it has not reached final approval, parts of it are already supported by Microsoft and other identity solution providers (tinyurl.com/7nzlg8p). Until identity providers are more broadly deployed the only practical solution is federated identity. Stay tuned for more on web SSO in the near future.

6.10 Cloud Accessible Authentication Directory

As applications are placed in the cloud, the need for the databases to support those applications implies that access to the data will be available to the cloud. There will be little incentive to keep the database on-premises if any significant application for the database is in the cloud.

Authentication data is a good example. The authoritative source of the authentication information is typically some HR or customer database that is synchronized with one or more IT directory servers. While it's customary for the directory servers to be on-premises, it is a good idea to examine the need for authentication to cloud resources. For example, if email servers are to be provisioned in the cloud, then the implication is that the address list will also be in cloud.

Once that decision is made there is no longer much of a privacy implication to putting the entire organizational directory server in the cloud as well. The cautionary result of any decision to move applications to the cloud is that database requirements will migrate to the cloud as well. Once access to the database is enabled from the cloud, there is little reason not to move the database itself to the cloud and allow on-premises application access. As an optimization, read-only copies of any directory service will support faster response and resilience in the loss of network connectivity.

6.11   Cloud Accessible Authorization

If cloud accessible authentication information is not politically acceptable, then some other method for authorizing access in the cloud needs to be enabled. When authorization claims are demanded by relying servers in the cloud, the local policy can make just-in-time decisions about which data is permitted on a case-by-case basis. The SAML and OAuth2 standards have some of that capability today, but a general solution is awaiting the completion of a protocol that will enable a business model for identity providers.

Until then a federated solution with data release policy applied to each federated organization is the only solution. The key to broader availability of selective disclosure is choosing an identity provider, so that is the decision that needs the most attention as the organization moves its resource into the cloud. The reality is that SAML has only been adopted by 10-20 percent of the market according to Forrester, Gartner, and others. OpenID and HTTP Federation are also very useful in federating the widest range of existing user stores and SAAS applications.

6.12   Summary: Three Steps to Prepare

Cloud services will be part of the future of every IT department sooner or later, it is critical for the IT professional to get ahead of the coming onslaught. Three areas will need the most attention in advance of any move into the cloud.

1.   Management of the hybrid cloud is an evolving area that will need the most attention because it is currently the least understood. Try to spend some time exploring management tools like System Center App Controller.

2.   User authentication and directory services will be needed anywhere that employees or other users expect to access organization resources. Since some governments have strict rules about the locations of private data, try to determine where the authoritative data will reside and how it will be migrated to the other clouds that need it.

3.   Access control and data leak prevention will become more difficult as data migrates to the cloud. As a goal, a role-based access control mechanism base on SAML claims seems to be the best bet today for providing the required functionality.

Proactivity is the key for retaining control. Microsoft and HP (and presumably other OEMs) are planning on offering Azure-in-a-box—basically, approved server hardware for running Azure on-premises. This will be an interesting development in addressing the security and compliance concerns in cloud computing.

7 CONCLUSION

The most competitive businesses are not those that blindly follow trends. Many IT organizations still operate core services such as email, file storage, and the company's public website entirely in-house. And some of those companies retain better control of their data by keeping it on-premises. But those companies are the minority: the threat landscape for Internet-accessible data changes so quickly that few organizations can afford to keep up. The fact is that data must be accessible, and therefore at risk, in order to be useful. The goal of IT is not only to be a facilitator and an enabler – supporting existing business needs – but also to harness technology in a way that new business capabilities become possible. Those that fail to invest the resources necessary to understand the potential of cloud computing will inevitably be surpassed by those competitors that habitually take the time to understand new technologies.

What does cloud computing offer? In a nutshell: rapid deployment of new line of business capabilities, efficient scale up and scale down, OpEx pricing, outsourcing of non-core skills, and bulk purchasing of commodity infrastructure. Some of the opportunities are obvious: few companies have any strategic reason for building their own Internet content distribution network, for example. Likewise, Internet email and file sharing services operate at such scale that the cost of duplicating them is tough to justify.

But cloud computing offers strategic opportunities as well: capabilities for innovation that go beyond the constant pressure on IT to cut costs. These opportunities include more natural support for mobile computing, collaboration and federation with partners and customers, and the ability to quickly deploy and update apps as business needs evolve. Identifying those opportunities is less about hopping on the cloud computing bandwagon than it is about training and planning.

Security is a topic that must be included during the IT planning phase; it doesn't work to address it retroactively after deployment – it inevitably becomes expensive and cumbersome at that point. But when security capabilities are designed into a solution from the beginning, they become an enabler. The collaboration and federation opportunities mentioned above are good examples in that they're realized primarily via authentication and authorization technologies.

Collaboration and federation are also good examples of where the effective use of cloud infrastructure currently requires additional investment in control. That is, controlling and measuring who has access to what resources is tough in any sufficiently complex IT environment, even self-contained on-premises ones. Mobile computing and the "bring your own device" trend have made this even harder: users are accessing a variety of Internet resources from a variety of unmanaged client devices. Access control in this dispersed, heterogeneous environment is tough to manage and this is an area in which many security technology vendors are currently investing.

Taking advantage of these new tools won't require a quantum leap in IT staffing capability. After all, the best people have always been those that invest in their careers and adapt. Indeed, the use of cloud computing lends itself to small, nimble IT organizations. Furthermore, the same security paradigms – authentication, authorization, auditing – still apply, regardless of where a system is running and who's running it, and technology vendors have incentive to create infrastructure management tools that behave consistently.

I challenge you to think of one software application or IT capability that would make your business more efficient. Could any part of it be quickly deployed to the cloud as a low-risk proof of concept? What combination of authentication and encryption tools are required to make that application secure? By routinely performing such an exercise, and committing resources to experimenting with the cloud in that way, your IT organization will be viewed as a strategic asset to the business, and a resource for innovative solutions.

ABOUT THE AUTHOR

Dan Griffin is the President of JW Secure, Inc. located in Seattle, WA. Founded in 2006, JW Secure specializes in custom security software development.